Who is bought and sold?

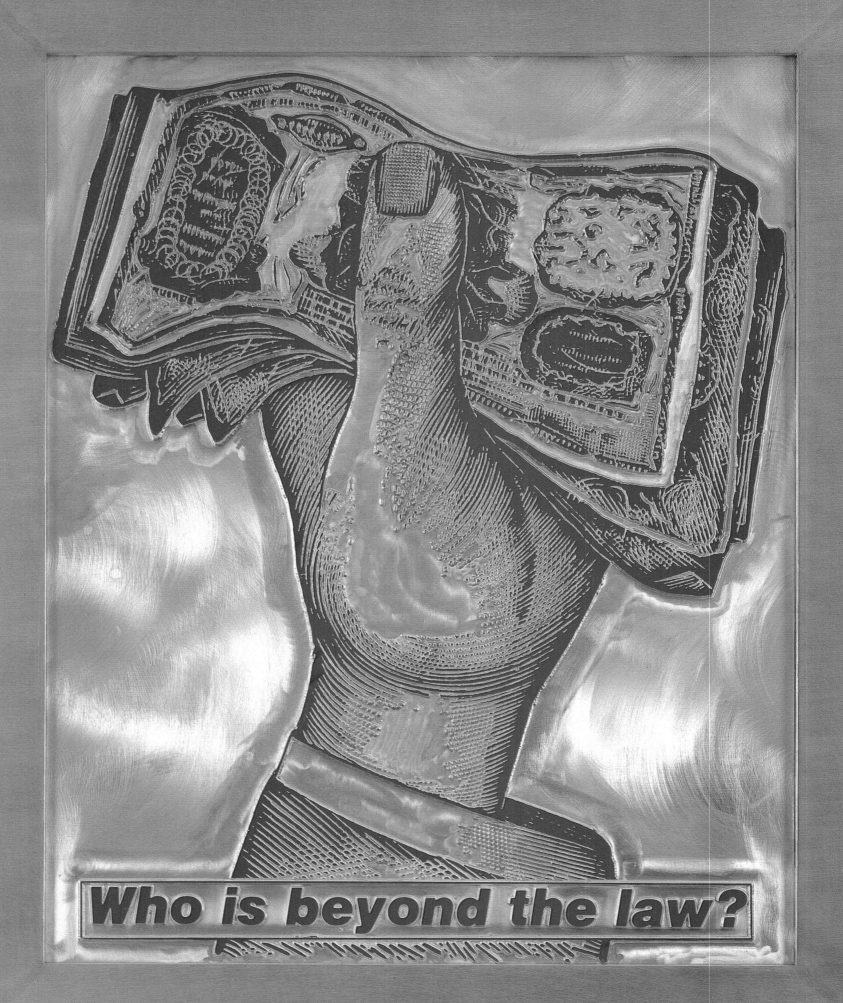

Love for Sale

The Words and Pictures of Barbara Kruger
Text by Kate Linker

Harry N. Abrams, Inc., Publishers

Editor: Charles Miers
Designer: Samuel N. Antupit
Editorial Assistant: Ellen Rosefsky
Design Assistant: E. Nygaard Ford

Library of Congress Cataloging-in-Publication Data
Kruger, Barbara, 1945–
Love for sale: the words and pictures of
 Barbara Kruger / text by Kate Linker
  p.   cm.
 Includes bibliographical references.
 ISBN 0-8109-2651-2
 1. Kruger, Barbara, 1945–   —Themes, motives.
I. Linker, Kate.
II. Title.
N6537.K78A4   1990
  700'.92–dc20   89–28321

Paperback edition published in 1996 by
Harry N. Abrams, Incorporated, New York
A Times Mirror Company

Clothbound edition published in 1990 by
Harry N. Abrams, Inc.

Printed in Japan

The publisher gratefully acknowledges
Ron Warren and the Mary Boone Gallery,
New York, for assistance with photographic
research and for providing photographs

Works of art on the following pages were
photographed by Zindman/Fremont, New
York: 1–8; 20, 21, 26, 37, 39, 41, 55–57, 89,
92–96. Photographs on pages 30, 64, and 80
courtesy Enrique Cubillo

Plates, pages 1–8:

UNTITLED (WHO IS BOUGHT AND SOLD?). 1989.
Photoengraving on magnesium, 25½ × 21½".
Sadoff Collection

UNTITLED (WHO IS BEYOND THE LAW?). 1989.
Photoengraving on magnesium, 25½ × 21½".
Sadoff Collection

UNTITLED (WHO IS FREE TO CHOOSE?). 1989.
Photoengraving on magnesium, 25½ × 21½".
Collection Mr. and Mrs. Howard L. Ganek,
New York

UNTITLED (WHO FOLLOWS ORDERS?). 1989.
Photoengraving on magnesium, 25½ × 21½".
Courtesy Mary Boone Gallery, New York

UNTITLED (WHO SALUTES LONGEST?). 1989.
Photoengraving on magnesium, 25½ × 21½".
Courtesy Mary Boone Gallery, New York

UNTITLED (WHO PRAYS LOUDEST?). 1989.
Photoengraving on magnesium, 25½ × 21½".
Collection of Alan Hergott and Curt Shepard

UNTITLED (WHO DIES FIRST?). 1989.
Photoengraving on magnesium, 25½ x 21½".
Collection of Alan Hergott and Curt Shepard

UNTITLED (WHO LAUGHS LAST?). 1989.
Photoengraving on magnesium, 25½ × 21½".
Courtesy Mary Boone Gallery, New York

Plates, pages 89–96:

HEART (DO I HAVE TO GIVE UP ME TO BE LOVED BY YOU?). 1988.
Photographic silkscreen on vinyl, 111½ × 111½".
Collection Emily Fisher Landau, New York

SURVEILLANCE IS YOUR BUSYWORK. 1985.
Billboard project organized by Film in the Cities
and First Banks, Minneapolis

UNTITLED (MY HERO). 1986.
Lenticular photograph, 19 × 19".
Courtesy Mary Boone Gallery, New York

UNTITLED (WE DECORATE YOUR LIFE). 1985.
Lenticular photograph, 19 × 19".
Courtesy Mary Boone Gallery, New York

UNTITLED (HELP! I'M LOCKED INSIDE THIS PICTURE). 1985.
Lenticular photograph, 20 × 20".
Courtesy Mary Boone Gallery, New York

UNTITLED (THERE IS ONLY ONE ANTIDOTE TO MENTAL SUFFERING AND THAT IS PHYSICAL PAIN). 1988.
Photoengravings on magnesium, 24 x 20" each (6).
Collection Vijak Mahdavi and Bernardo Nadal-Ginard

UNTITLED (YOU GET AWAY WITH MURDER). 1987.
Photograph, 30¼ × 30".
Collection Beatrice and Philip Gersh, Beverly Hills,
California

UNTITLED (GIVE ME ALL YOU'VE GOT). 1986.
Photograph, 48 × 60".
Collection Dennis and Ellen Schweber

UNTITLED (JAM LIFE INTO DEATH). 1988.
Photographic silkscreen on vinyl, 111½ × 111½".
Collection Ydessa Hendeles Art Foundation,
Toronto

UNTITLED (REMEMBER ME). 1988.
Photographic silkscreen on vinyl, 149 × 105½".
Courtesy Mary Boone Gallery, New York

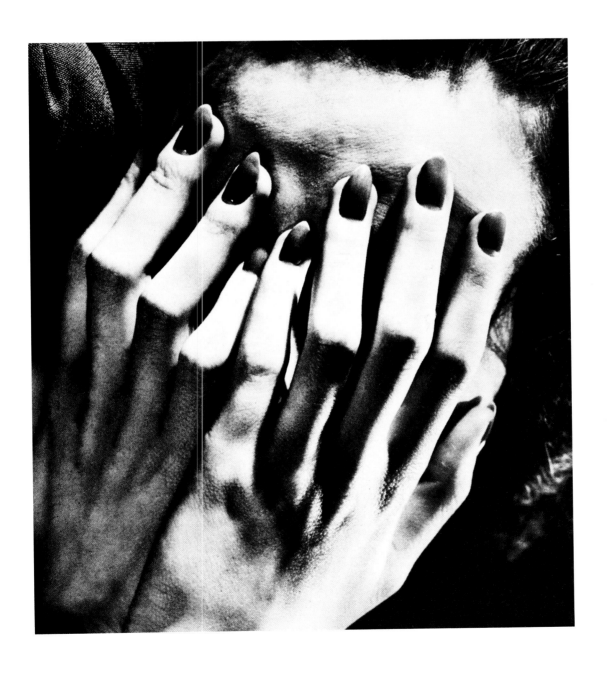

Contents

For nearly a decade Barbara Kruger has made provocative objects: pictures that entice and beguile only to accost us with accusatory words. Typically large, her works incorporate photographs taken from different media sources that she has cropped, enlarged, and juxtaposed with strident verbal statements or phrases. Art historically, these works belong to the realm of montage, but they resist the smooth coherence associated with that genre. For there is no complacency to her art, which is assertive, aggressive, and argumentative. Kruger's is an art of interference, of semiotic conflict.

Kruger's practice reflects the discovery, evident throughout contemporary art, of the formative power of images, the capacity of signs to affect deep structures of belief. However, she applies this realization to a political agenda. Her art is concerned with the positioning of the social body, with the ways in which our thoughts, attitudes, and desires are determined by society's dictates. Through her arsenal of visual devices, Kruger proposes to intervene in stereotypical representations, disrupting their power, displacing their hold, and clearing a space for enlightened awareness. To this end, she operates within the multiple sites through which signs circulate, producing books, posters, and billboards as well as such popular consumer objects as T-shirts and matchbooks. Her works demonstrate the intrusion of the public into the private, much as they mingle major and minor media. They attend to the peregrinations of power, as it places, positions, imposes.

In consequence of these activities, Kruger is at once a social commentator and a political agitator. Her work has both a place and a strategic role within contemporary artistic discourse. On one hand, it testifies to the recent broadening of artistic practice, pointing to the expansion of culture into politics. But it also evinces changes, wrought in the last two decades, that are inextricably linked to the phenomenon of the postmodern. For Kruger, as for many contemporary theorists, postmodernism is not a style succeeding the dissolution of modernism but rather a historical condition, marked by new philosophical relations; it signals a rupture with the notion of sovereign and transcendent individuality inherited from the Enlightenment. The postmodern self is not the centered and controlling subject, set apart from and "master" over history; indeed, inasmuch as postmodernism emphasizes the regulating power of social forces, it can be said to describe the decentering of the self. Its major focus is less the modernist theme of the creative subject of production than the production of the subject, for it inquires into the ways in which our identities are constructed by representations in society. Kruger investigates the underside of this process, examining how representation legislates, defines, *subjects*.

Kruger's art exhibits other features that are trademarks of postmodernist practice. Like many of her generation, she develops images by reproducing other images, appropriating the media's picturings so as to extend and amplify their rhetoric. Her wily manipulations elude aesthetic categorization: no formal criteria can explain them, just as they do not lodge easily within the established traditions of posters, art photography, and so on. In a characteristically postmodernist manner, she erodes classifications, merging images and words, multiplying media, and annexing concepts from other disciplines.

In Kruger's art this process is extended, for hers is a "splintered" practice that avoids the unity and integrity that are common to an artist's *oeuvre*. In addition to her customary role, Kruger has occupied the positions of editor, curator, teacher, and organizer of lectures; she is also an accomplished writer who has been the monthly film critic for *Artforum* since 1982 and, since 1987, the author of the magazine's television column. Her conventional activities as an artist are augmented by her work as a designer of posters, book covers, and announcements for political groups, individuals, and institutions. Most recently, Kruger has engaged with architects and landscape designers in collaborative projects for highly innovative parks. These activities are not supplemental, but rather fundamental, to a practice that courts multiplicity of sites and meanings. It is a practice that, characteristically, begins elsewhere, *outside* the artistic frame.

Early Work

D iscussions of Kruger's background yield few facts, since she frowns at established historiographic techniques; her key influences, she notes, can be found in movies, television, and the stereotypical situations of everyday life.[1] Kruger was born in Newark, New Jersey, in 1945, the only child in a lower middle-class family.[2] Her mother was a legal secretary, her father a chemical technician who worked for several companies before settling down with Shell Oil in Union, New Jersey. Kruger attended Weequahic High School, then enrolled at Syracuse University in 1964, only to return home one year later, when her father died.

In 1965 Kruger began classes at Parsons School of Design, where she concentrated in the fine arts program. At the time, Parsons' curriculum was conservative, but Kruger was fortunate to have Diane Arbus and Marvin Israel as teachers. Arbus

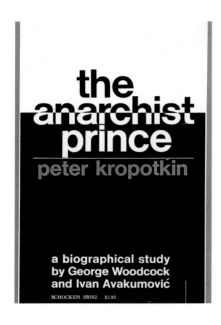

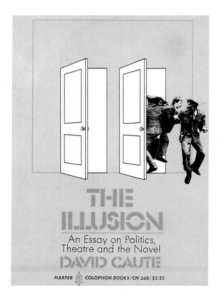

was important not only as an example of a significant female artist but also as one of the few photographers to expose the complex, seamy (and, to Arbus, totally fascinating) underside of suburban life. But the primary influence on Kruger was exerted by Israel, a noted graphic designer and art director of *Harper's Bazaar* in the early 1960s. Israel took a personal interest in Kruger, encouraging her talents, introducing her to photographers and, in general, exposing her to the rapidly expanding world of fashion magazines, which formed one of the decade's salient cultural developments. When Kruger's interest in art school lagged in the mid-1960s, Israel encouraged her to assemble a professional design portfolio.

Soon Kruger took her portfolio to Condé Nast Publications, where she was given a job at *Mademoiselle*. She began by designing small box-shaped advertisements for mail-order products located at the back of the magazine but was promoted to chief designer within a year. As Carol Squiers has observed, Kruger, "at the age of 22 . . . was single-handedly designing a national fashion magazine"[3]—a considerable accomplishment for one with little professional experience. At the same time she began free-lance work designing covers for books that, interestingly, were largely political texts.

Kruger describes her experience as a graphic designer as "the biggest influence on my work," noting that it "became, with a few adjustments, my 'work' as an artist." The experience informs her art on several levels. One might be called the level of procedures, evident in Kruger's sharp eye for scanning and selecting images, gauging their rhetorical potential, and then adjusting sizes and cropping dimensions so as to focus their visual impact. This repertory of devices is the stock-in-trade of the skilled designer, but it has no parallel in the formal manipulations of the traditional artist. More subtle and insidious, however, is the strategic level, manifest in advertising's choreography of seduction, or what Kruger terms its "brand of exhortation and entrapment." In fashion advertising, Kruger found a means to "hail" and engage the viewer, forcing attention to an image's innuendos. As Kruger has observed, "This 'hailing' . . . is one of the prominent tactics of most public design work, whether it be advertising, corporate signage, or editorial design. In all this work, the economy of the overture is central and involves all manner of shortcuts which waste no words." Or, as she has elaborated: "I learned to deal with an economy of image and text which beckoned and fixed the spectator. I learned to think about a kind of quickened effectivity, an accelerated seeing and reading which reaches a near apotheosis in television."

When Kruger turned to the art world in 1969, it was to a sphere in flux, distinguished by the waning hold of Pop and Minimalism and by the initial manifestations of Conceptual Art. Most decisively, it was to a masculine terrain which had not experienced the social transformations of the 1970s that would give new impetus to feminist practice. Kruger's first efforts as an artist reflect insecurity, unease, and (in her words) "alienation" deriving from her background in another discipline. Indeed, her early pieces, large woven hangings, pertain more to the realm of craft and to a kind of feminist work as yet little known in America. The stitching, crocheting, and weaving in this art (conventional "women's work," or, Kruger notes, activity that was "allowed" to women) erupted in whimsical patterns of brightly patterned cloth laced with metallic yarns and rows of sequins, ribbons, and feathers. Kruger soon quit her job, although she continued to support herself and her art through free-lance work as a picture editor. But she was increasingly drawn to New York's poetry world and to the intrusion of the word into visual art that was manifest in the antiformal impulses of 1970s narrative art and performance. She began writing poems, attending poetry readings and giving her own readings, and publishing her poetry in a little-known magazine, *Tracks, a journal of artists writings*. Hesitation was also evident in her visual art; for a year she dabbled in painting.

By this time Kruger had moved into a large, spare downtown loft that would be the locus of her art making and writing for some twenty years. She had also begun to establish a reputation in the art world. Her stitch-and-glitter-encrusted painting, *2 a.m. Cookie*, was included in the Whitney *Biennial* in 1973, and she had two one-person exhibitions in New York, the first at the alternative gallery Artists' Space in 1974, the second at the Fischbach Gallery in 1975. But she was becoming listless with her practice, which increasingly seemed a mere "potpourri of decorative exercises." She was also troubled by the work's detachment from her life and from the social and political issues that were becoming her concern. For Kruger was aware that much radical thinking of the 1970s required investigating the social nature of artistic production and reception, inquiring into the role of institutions, cultural conventions, and codes in determining the meaning of works of art. In the fall of 1976 she left New York for the University of California at Berkeley, to take up the first in a series of teaching stints that would occupy her for a four-year period.

In California, Kruger abandoned artmaking for a year and spent her time reading, driving, going to movies, and, as she puts it, trying "to rethink my connections to my work, to the art world, and most importantly, to the games and relations that congeal, disperse and make the world go round." Kruger's comments are, of course, retrospective, but they point to a growing attention to the complex of social and political activities that make up "real life." When she returned to making art, it was not to the manual labor of handicraft but to picture taking, to photographing

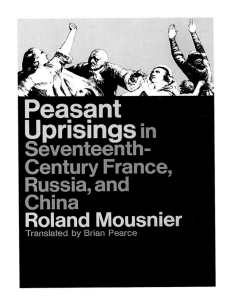

Book covers designed by Barbara Kruger:
THE ANARCHIST PRINCE. 1971.
8 × 5½".
Courtesy Schocken Books, New York
THE ILLUSION. 1972.
8 × 5½".
Courtesy Harper/Colophon Books, New York
PEASANT UPRISINGS. 1972.
8 × 5½".
Courtesy Harper Torchbooks, New York
CAPITALISM IN ARGENTINE CULTURE. 1971.
8 × 5½".
Courtesy University of Pennsylvania Press, Philadelphia

The manipulation of the object
The blaming of the victim
The accusation of hysteria
The making mute

No

residential buildings in California in a deadpan, if somewhat lapidary, manner. These photographs bear a superficial resemblance to the early serial images of Ed Ruscha. In 1977 she published them in an artist's book entitled *Picture/Readings*, placing the photographs opposite short narratives she wrote that hinted at possible thoughts and actions of the building's inhabitants. For the first time in her art, image and text play contrapuntally; the written texts do not so much oppose a "lived" interior with an exterior form as they make sensible or audible elements that remained unseen and unheard, hinting at architecture's power over social activity.

Social relations as experienced in everyday activities dominate Kruger's work of the next few years. She addressed this theme in various modes and media, continuing the double-panel format or composing installations and performances employing slide projections and audiotapes or live readings. A group of four-panel works entitled the "Hospital Series" is indicative of her later production (page 16). Here, image and text are still arranged in disparate panels: the first panel showing photographic details of hospital fixtures; the third, images—now appropriated from other sources—of social situations. But in the second panel are cryptically evocative phrases—"the elimination of the romantic body," "the honing of the functional gesture"—that hint at Kruger's suggestive word use to come. In the last panel, language is reduced to a short phrase or word: "Please," "No," "Not that." Although the relations between the different panels are too elusive to trigger a sustained reaction, the heightened economy of the devices points toward Kruger's mature style. By using language and images derived from other sources, Kruger was developing a culturally informed practice that eliminated the personal elements of art making. In a group of photocollages made in 1979 and 1980, appropriated images are overlaid with phrases or words (page 16). In one, a policeman eyes a man in a coat and tie and the text reads "Business"; in another, an image of a woman surrounded by fashion magazines is stamped with the word "Deluded"; a third work that spells out "Perfect" shows a hierarchically posed photograph of a woman, her hands clasped in prayer. Rectangular planes of color and solid and dotted lines score the surfaces with marks of the designer's trade. The implications of the works are political, social, feminist.

The technology of early death
The providing of consumer goods to a dying populace
The manufacture of plague
The denial of epidemic

No don't

By the late 1970's Kruger had become associated with a group of artists that included Ross Bleckner, Barbara Bloom, and David Salle, all of whom were educated at the California Institute of the Arts, the training ground for much acclaimed contemporary practice. To this list should be added Richard Prince, Jenny Holzer, Cindy Sherman, Sarah Charlesworth, and Sherrie Levine, among others, who were developing what Kruger calls "a vernacular sort of signage." At issue for these artists were not only the strategies of media presentation but also the reality of mediation, or rather, the hold on the real exerted by the plural signs circulating in society. Indeed, many of them were drawn to semiotics, the "science of signs" propounded by such European cultural theorists as Jean Baudrillard and Roland Barthes. However, most of these artists were concerned with exposing the supposed neutrality of signs and examining the regimes of meaning established through representation. Kruger notes the importance of the exhibition "Pictures," organized by critic Douglas Crimp for Artists' Space in 1977, which dealt with representation as constructing reality.

This interest is evident in "Pictures and Promises. A Display of Advertisings, Slogans, and Interventions," which Kruger herself curated for the Kitchen Center for Video and Music in early 1981 (page 17). The language of the accompanying press release is now typically Kruger's, as are the strategies outlined. Delineating the scope of her inclusions ("magazine and newspaper advertisements, artists' works, television commercials, posters, 'commercial' photography, corporate insignia and public signage"), Kruger remarked on contemporary artists' "demystification" of "popular visual language," describing the critical shift effected by repositioning social discourse: "The quotational qualities of these words and pictures remove them and their 'originals' from the seemingly natural position within the flow of dominant social directives, into the realm of commentary." The diction ("seemingly natural," "dominant social directives") strikes at characteristic themes of the artist's mature work. Elsewhere, she remarked on how the appropriation of devices from the media permitted a counter to its fascinating promises, affording "a doubled address, a coupling of the ingratiation of wishful thinking with the criticality of knowing better." Kruger's distinctive strategy is encapsulated: seduce, then intercept.

Plates, page 16:

HOSPITAL. 1978.
  Photograph and text, 19¼ × 48".

UNTITLED (DELUDED). 1979.
  Photograph, 32 × 32".
  Photograph courtesy D. James Dee

UNTITLED (DUAL). 1979.
  Photograph, 32 × 32".
  Collection Ross Bleckner.
  Photograph courtesy D. James Dee

UNTITLED (PERFECT). 1980.
  Photoprint, type on paper, 37¾ × 37¾".
  Collection Henry S. McNeil, Jr., Philadelphia

Plates, page 17:

HOSPITAL. 1978.
  Photograph and text, 19¼ × 48".

PICTURES AND PROMISES. 1980.
  Exhibition curated by Barbara Kruger.
  Installation view, The Kitchen, New York.
  Photograph by Paula Court

In 1981 Kruger was included in "Public Address," a group show held at the Annina Nosei Gallery. The exhibited pieces, along with concurrent work, bear what has become her trademark "look." Red enameled frames enclose sharp black-and-white images culled from old photographic annuals, instruction manuals, and magazines and overlaid with phrases set in blocks of bold-faced type. The planarity of the imagery simulates the two-dimensionality of printed media, while their sharp foregrounding has an expository quality, a visual punch that assaults the viewer. Kruger's words are explicit, impertinent, declarative. In one piece (page 68), a shadowy picture of well-shod feet is confronted with the charge "You make history when you do business"; in another, the chasm separating a man's face from a woman's is inundated by a cascade of incriminating words: "You destroy what you think is difference." A third work (page 53) shows the mushroom cloud of a nuclear explosion and bears the caption "Your manias become science." In the ensuing years Kruger would circulate these images outside of conventional venues; thus, when she was included among the few women invited to exhibit in the prestigious *Documenta VII* art fair in Kassel, West Germany, in 1982, she distributed posters spelling out the slogan "Your moments of joy have the precision of military strategy" throughout the town (page 52). And increasingly Kruger would intercept the flow of signs within different channels of distribution, using both large public billboards (and the Times Square spectacolor sign; page 27) as well as the more intimate form of books. With astonishing rapidity, Kruger expanded her focus to address the global etiquettes of power.

You invest in the

divinity

of the masterpiece

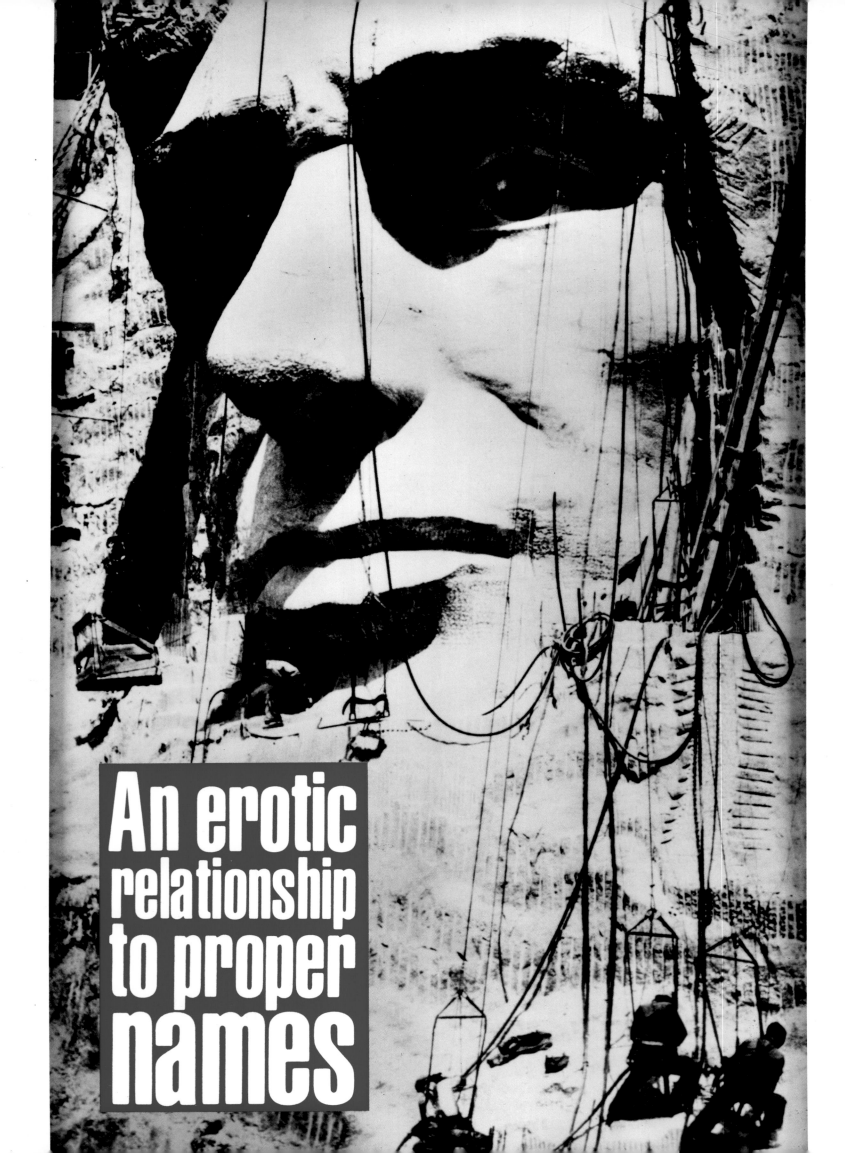

An erotic
relationship
to proper
names

choose the Impres...
unity and intensity
...ion of alternate...
parts of any pictur...
o real picture at all
whole composition...
vised apprehension
t experiences, and
appeal to visual or
tamination, a false
t which is actually
art should be self...
sthetes of modern

Has not Walter
ll the arts aspire
ect is the Impress...

take sides. Ev...
end on concen...
to be attained
al beauties of
lines. To put
Chardin did, as
in the keenest
this may not
operly affords.
memories, of
e more highly
thetized than
ut of a com-

plex of vision and memory and must itself be complex.
It took time and analysis to paint John
extra **You** ...ry decoration of the Sacrame *are* ent's
take ...and analysis to appreciate it. It will not
bloom gradu... ...ne's passive vision like a cathe-
dral front ...a ...*motion*...onet, for its appeal is both
visual a... posite vis...ry must be adjusted into a
of sight a... nd the parallel experiences
ki... o... t in the tas...etr *giving* spectator, as
y the... In fac...e le*gitimac*...rea the old-fashioned way of
king in... picture—w...s ould be clearly distin-
gui...ed fr... ling that is destructive
of all pic... a mere cas... legitimacy is best vin-
dicated by... effect— ... the spectator does in epitome
and **US** hout...ng tha... error. When... the artist ...d by
process of tri...nd error. ...in the...ne
...s's staircase decor...
Public Library, ...el their large...*ty, then,* w...n
general impressi... still in the co... of *my eye,* ol...
the lovely and... ...tful detai...nd *the articul*...
of the pa... ...and t...n *come back*
enha... ...ation to the whol...
I ... repeati *evil* e creati... when I do this
P... with a clear but in...rocess by w...
the...
i *the* di... ...d the parts until...lete visi...
until once mo... ...nes and ri... art...tion,
completed, stood forth in its destined beauty *eye*
Indeed is not such a process of appreciation and

I pledge allegiance to the flag of the United States of America and to the Republic for which it stands, one nation under God, indivisible, with liberty and justice for all.

I take you, to have and to hold, from this day forward, for better for worse, for richer for poorer, in sickness and in health, to love and to cherish, till death do us part, so help me God.

I, being of sound mind and body, but also aware of the uncertainties of this life, do hereby make, publish and declare this instrument as and for my last will and testament.

Who is bought and sold? Who is beyond the law? Who is free to choose? Who follows orders? Who salutes longest? Who prays loudest? Who dies first? Who laughs last?

Language is legislation, speech is its code. . . . To utter a discourse is not, as is too often repeated, to communicate; it is to subjugate.

—Roland Barthes

Barbara Kruger's art depends on a broadened sense of the political and on a redefinition of the human subject as constructed by the very social forces over which it formerly claimed control. She develops these focuses through a concept of power, which, like that advanced by Michel Foucault and seconded by Roland Barthes, is opposed to the "traditional" interpretation of power as constituted or embodied in a sovereign, state, or juridical apparatus. To Kruger, power is not localized in specific institutions but is dispersed through a multiplicity of sites, operating in the range of discursive procedures that govern sexuality, morality, the family, education, and so on. Conceived in this manner, power cannot be centralized; rather, it is diffuse, decentralized, and, in consequence, anonymous: it exists less as a "body" than as a network of relations unifying social apparatuses and institutions.

According to Foucault, this power is a strategy operating through "dispositions, manoeuvres, tactics, techniques, functionings."[4] It subjects the individual as much as the social body; hence, "power relations . . . invest [the individual or group], mark it, train it, torture it, force it to carry out tasks, to perform ceremonies, to emit signs."[5] Foucault emphasizes that power is not exerted through physical violence but through symbolic effects and that its efficacy derives from the subtlety with which it penetrates the most delicate mechanisms of social exchange:

> What makes it accepted, is quite simply the fact that it does not simply weigh like a force which says no, but that it runs through, and it produces, things, it induces pleasure, it forms knowledge, it produces discourse; it must be considered as a productive network which runs through the entire body much more than a negative instrument whose function is repression.[6]

For Barthes, the instrument in which power is inscribed is language, just as for Bertolt Brecht it is the social rhetoric of gesture. For Kruger, power implements its impositions through the imagistic stereotype, the pose.

Kruger's attention, like Foucault's, is directed to the control and positioning of the social body, a control that is instrumental to society's aim of producing normalized subjects that can be inserted into its ideological, social, and economic orders.[7] In *Vision and Painting: The Logic of the Gaze*, the art historian Norman Bryson elaborated on the implications of Foucault's theme, arguing that in Western societies based on visual culture, physical control is an infrequent mode of subjection; authority

is invested in the signifier or sign, and recognition becomes the central mode of interaction. Bryson describes this mode of domination by systems as "managerial," noting that in it "the ruling group must justify its authority through cultural values and forms; management, rather than control, is the customary expression of authority

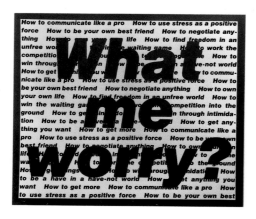

once overt and bodily subjection becomes impossible. The *entire* society must submit to these forms, if their regulatory intention is to become effective; a veiled exercise of power arises, through mechanisms that obey a new imperative: not to touch the body."[8] It is this "veiled" management of subjection, evident as much in fashion and entertainment as in other areas, that turns these separate spheres into an integrated public realm. Bryson concludes by noting that the "public acknowledgment of consensual fictions" is central to the "stability of the social formation."[9]

Kruger's mission is to erode the impassivity engendered by the imposition of social norms: hence the gist of a work from 1982, in which the statement "We have received orders not to move" is superimposed on an image of an immobile woman's body, pinned against a wall (page 28). The image is at once an invocation of social stasis and a feminist retort to the controlling structures of patriarchy, which perform the function—remarked on by Sigmund Freud—of getting woman into place. In another work from the same year, a counterfeit coin imprinted with the profiles of two men is overlaid with the slogan "Charisma is the perfume of your gods"—a statement that refers less to an explicitly feminist message than to the way in which the standardization of social currency is enacted by our subscription to society's suasions (page 29).

Kruger exposes the sterotype as the prime instrument of this submission, the ideological cliché that, Bryson observes, "knows . . . only one mode of address: exhortation."[10] To a degree, the stereotype is a component of all speech (which, Barthes remarks, comprehends "the authority of assertion" and the "gregariousness of repetition"[11]), and for this reason Barthes views language as invariably operating in the service of power. Kruger, though, approaches the stereotype in its most general semiotic meaning as a code, convention, or standard by which power is arbitrarily imposed. It is a means to subdue and, implicitly, to "decarnalize" the body; as Craig Owens observes, the stereotype's function is to "disavow agency; thus the body is dismantled as a locus of practice and reassembled as a discontinuous series of gestures and poses—that is, as a semiotic field."[12] The stereotype produces docile and submissive subjects, lacking any transformative capacity; hence Kruger refers to the stereotype's domain as that of "figures without bodies."

Throughout her art, the stereotype wears multiple guises, appearing as gesture (the handshake in *Admit nothing/Blame everyone/Be bitter*; page 51), as situation (*You make history when you do business*; page 53), or as a continuum of social commands (the run-on directives from a self-help book in *What me worry?*; page 28) and the political *idées reçues* in the *Pledge of Allegiance*; page 26). Often she invokes stereotypes in their most insinuating forms, as paradigms of identity that are socially inscribed rather than "chosen." Since much of Kruger's practice deals with representations of femininity, many works contest the peremptory imposition of masculine terms; hence she may contest the place assigned to women in her 1981 *You thrive on mistaken identity* or ironically propose "I am your reservoir of poses" (page 35).

Through her work Kruger aims to intercept the stereotype, to suspend the identification afforded by the gratifications of the image. To do this, she deploys the stereotype's "double address," by which it constructs the viewer twice over, addressing him or her both personally and impersonally, as individual (you, here . . .) and as type.[13] The stereotype makes use of the arsenal of its rhetorical powers to solicit and seduce, engaging the viewer through the particularities of its details, only to withdraw into the detached and disembodied reductions of the generalized image, the pose. In Kruger's hands these devices are both mimicked and arrested: she assumes the stereotype's exhortative techniques, employing its foregrounded, expository quality, only to block its fascinations through the intrusion of contrary and divisive texts. These relations of image and word contradict the conventions of the media, which tend to repeat an image's meaning either through captions (in the case of print media) or through a narrator's authoritative voice (in film). Thus, her devices serve to inhibit these pictures, to (in her words) "intercept the stunned silence of the image with the uncouth impertinences and uncool embarrassments of language."

Our current world is less a bureaucracy or even a technocracy than a mediacracy, in which the construction and management of society are controlled by the ever-extending sway of the media. Increasingly the media comprise distribution channels for orders. Kruger has remarked that coercion, today, is effected less through submission than through receivership, a state in which we consume the codes circulated by anonymous sources of power. Her statement points to the new importance accorded to consumption in the process of social incorporation; moreover, it suggests the role played by the media as the agent of mass repetition and reinforcement. For as the French writer Jacques Attali has observed, repetition functions as the arm of consumption to ensure both the diffusion and durability of power: "Possessing the means of recording allows one to monitor noises, to maintain them, and to control their repetition within a determined code. In the final analysis, it allows one to impose one's own noise and to silence others . . ." (Here Attali quotes Hitler: "Without the loudspeaker, we would never have conquered Germany."[14])

In various written texts Kruger has described her focus as "the panorama of social relations mediated by images," noting that the control once achieved through language has yielded to the picture—and, most recently, to pictures of electronic origin. Elsewhere she remarks that "the cool hum of power [resides] not in hot expulsions of verbiage, but in the elegantly mute thrall of sign language." Kruger's

Charisma is the perfume of your gods

What liberates metaphor, symbol, emblem, from poetic mania, what manifests its power of subversion, is the preposterous. The logical future of the metaphor would therefore be the gag.

—Roland Barthes

(Barthes by Barthes. New York: Hill and Wang, 1977)

Tragedy is if I cut my finger. Comedy is if I walk into a sewer and die.
—Mel Brooks

observations point to the tendency to reduce the plural spaces of lived life to surfaces, the shimmering expanses of the movie, television, or video screen, the billboard or magazine advertisement. As Jean Baudrillard comments, the reflexive spaces of humanism—scene and mirror—have been replaced by screen and network;[15] similarly, bodies give way to eviscerated figures, while the weight and substance of objects are abstracted into the beckoning visibility of commodities. This direction speaks to the tendency in Western society to privilege vision over other senses, intimating the eye's propensity for mastery, for captivation and control. Kruger's main concern is coercion achieved through that most prevalent form of imagery—the imagery of women.

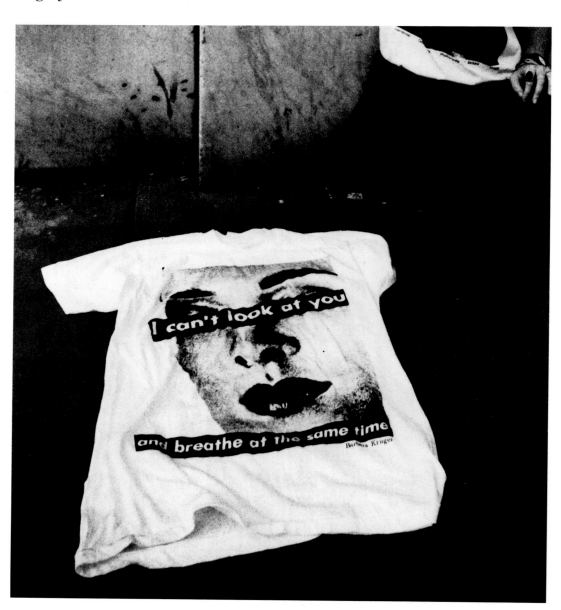

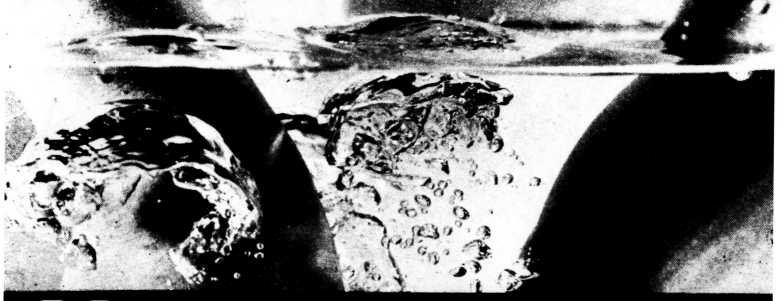

I am your

reservoir of poses

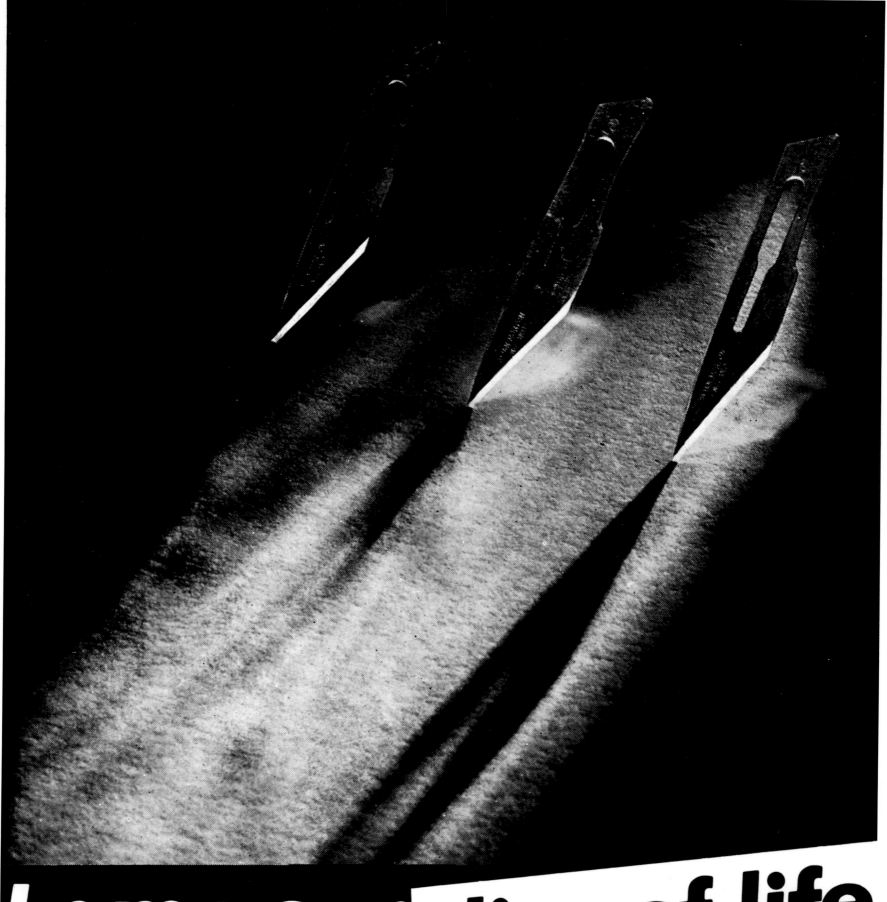

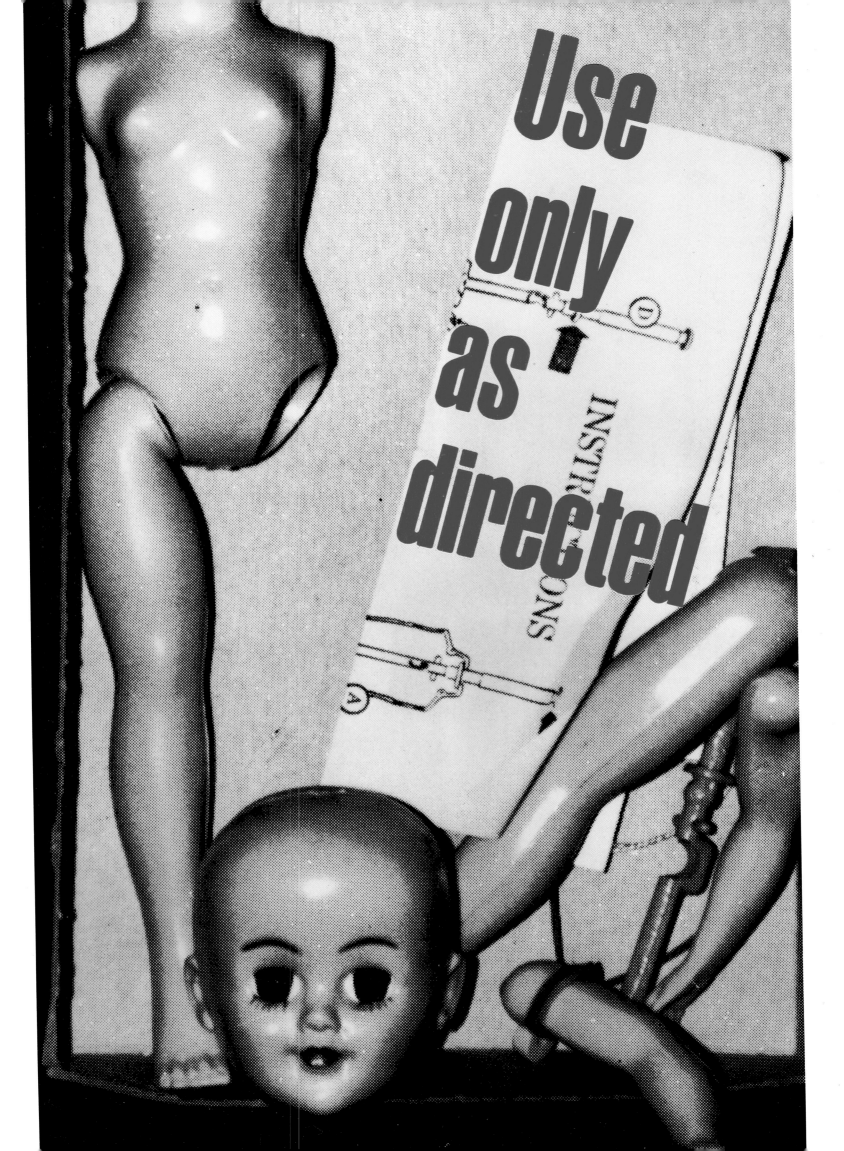

Use
only
as
directed

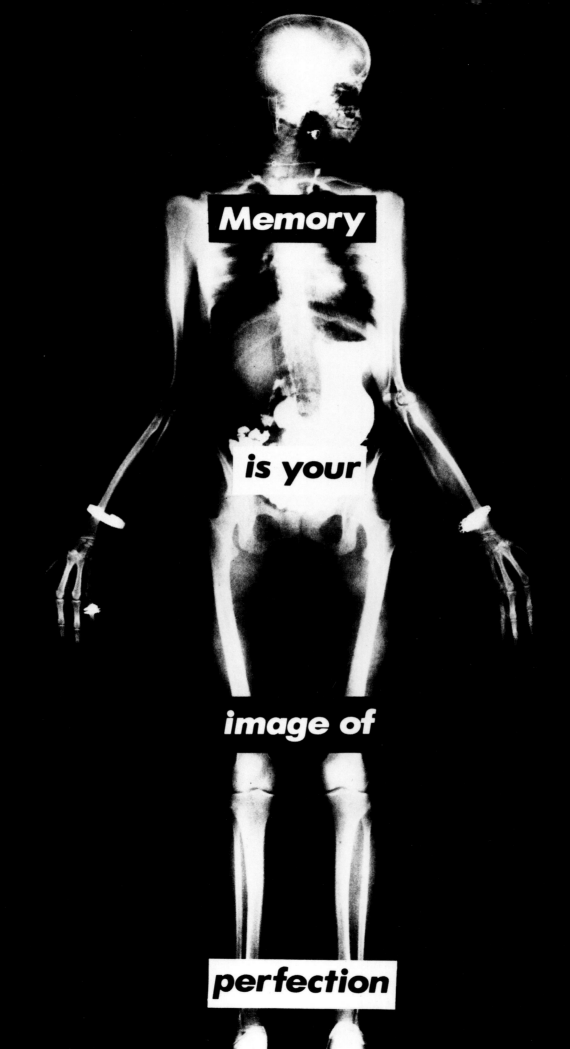

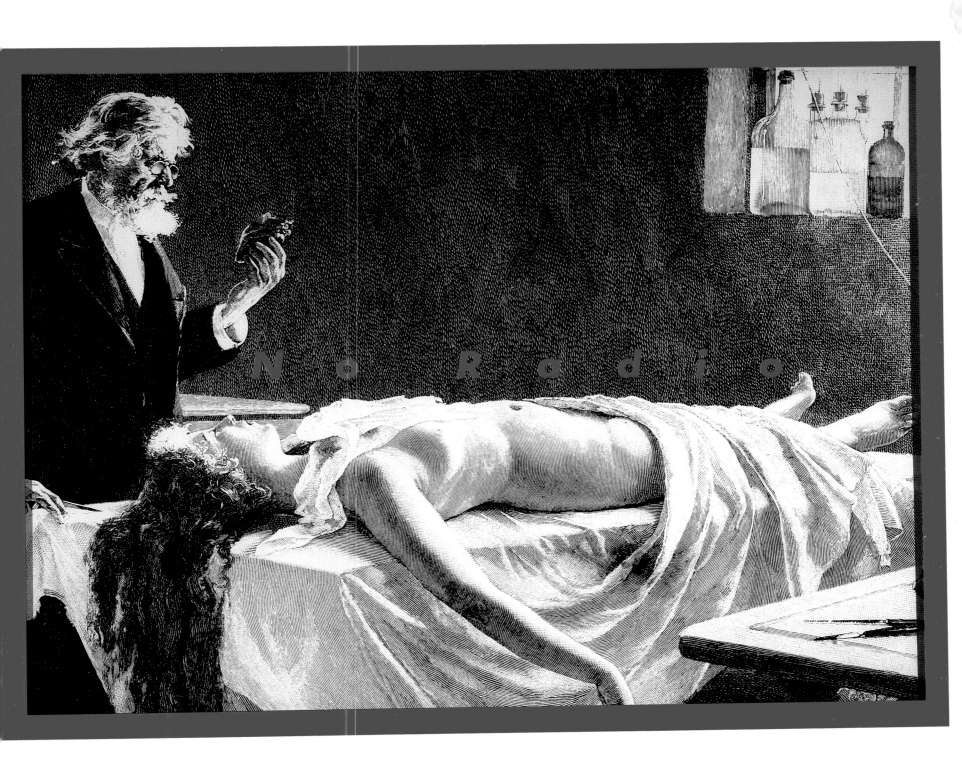

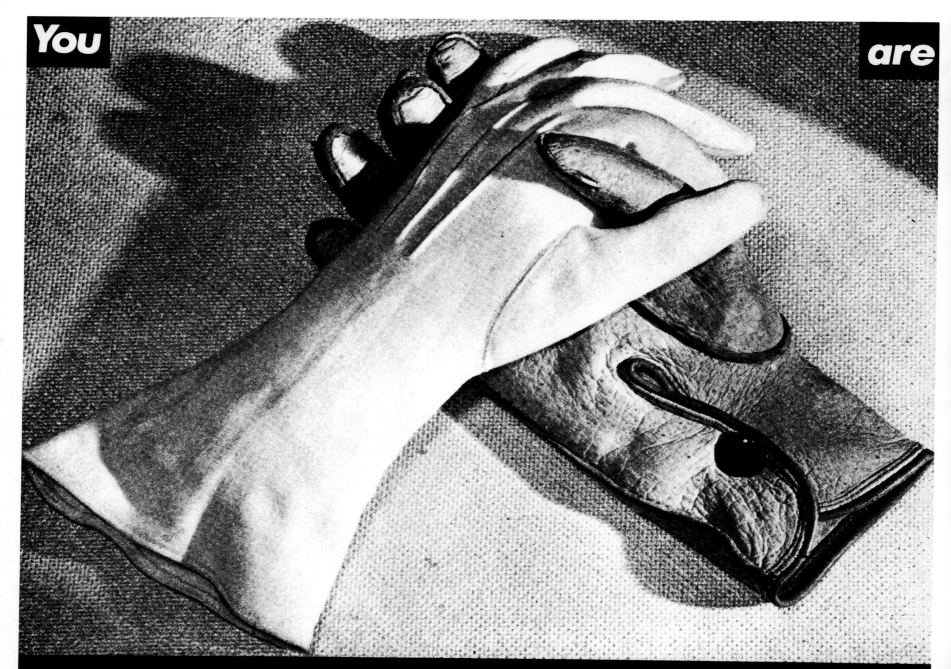

The marriage of Murder and Suicide

You are the perfect crime

My lordship   My lancelot   My crusader for peace with dignity
My Gipper   My chairman of the board   My guardian of culture
My provider   My host with the most   My host with the most   My baby mogul
My Rambo   My Popeye   My pimp   My doctor   My banker   My
lawyer   My landlord   My soldier of fortune   My provider   My
better half   My wunderkind   My quarterback   My top of the
charts   My great artist   My baby mogul   My sugar daddy   My
ticket to ride   My jack of all trades   My leader of the pack
My capo   My pope   My stickman   My ayatollah   My daddy
My lordship   My lancelot   My crusader for peace with dignity
My Gipper   My chairman of the board   My guardian of culture
My professor of desire   My host with the most   My Dagwood
My Rambo   My Popeye   My pimp   My doctor   My banker   My
lawyer   My landlord   My soldier of fortune   My provider
better half   My wunderkind   My quarterback   My top of the
charts   My great artist   My baby mogul   My sugar daddy   My
ticket to ride   My jack of all trades   My leader of the pack
My capo   My pope   My stickman   My ayatollah   My daddy

What big muscles you have!

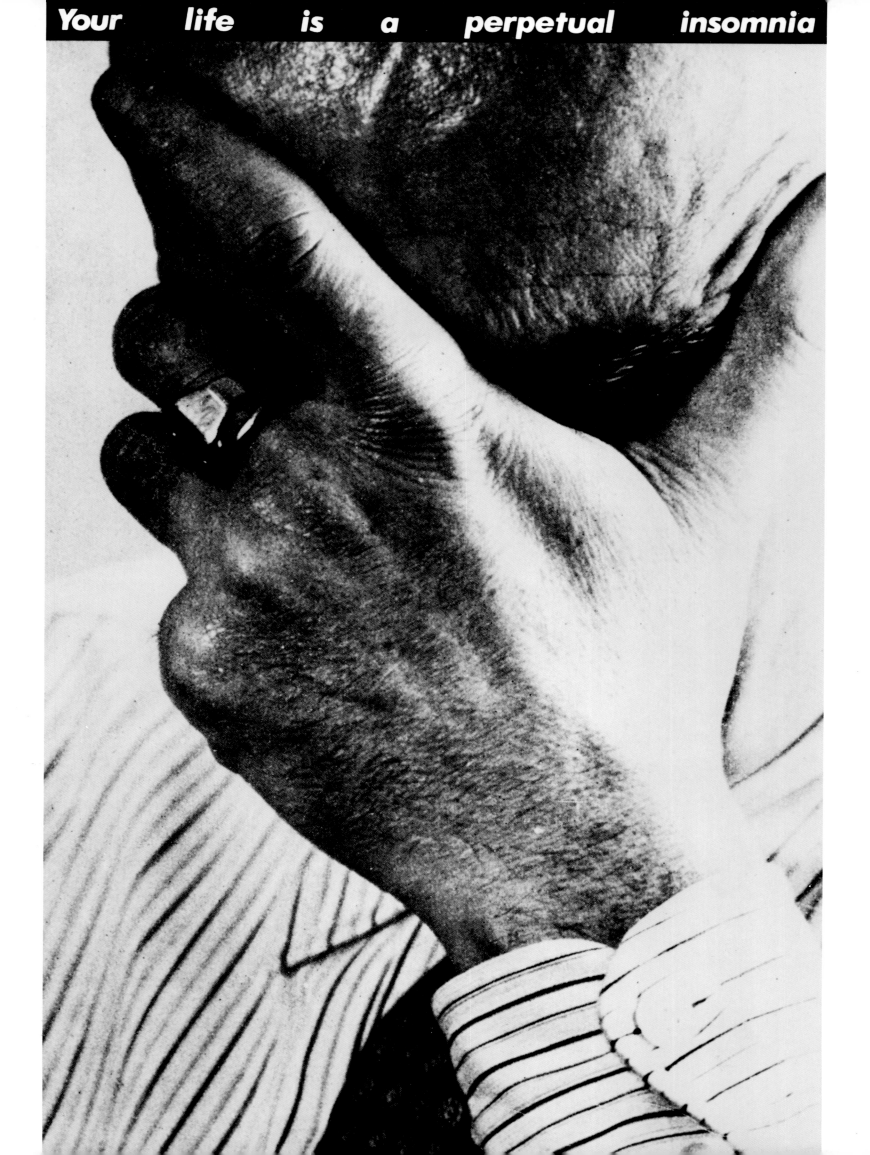

Your life is a perpetual insomnia

Busy going crazy

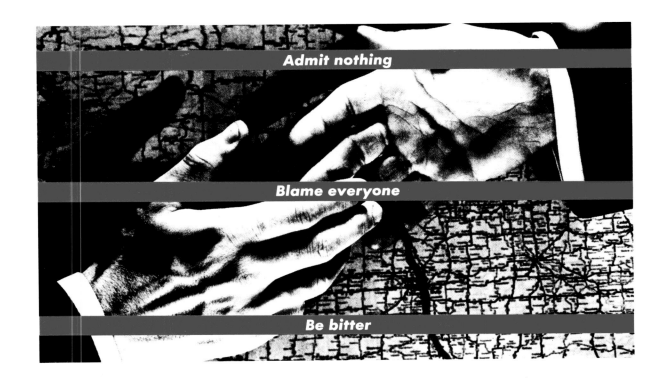

Admit nothing

Blame everyone

Be bitter

Endangered

species

We construct

the chorus

of missing persons

Your moments of joy have the precision of military strategy.

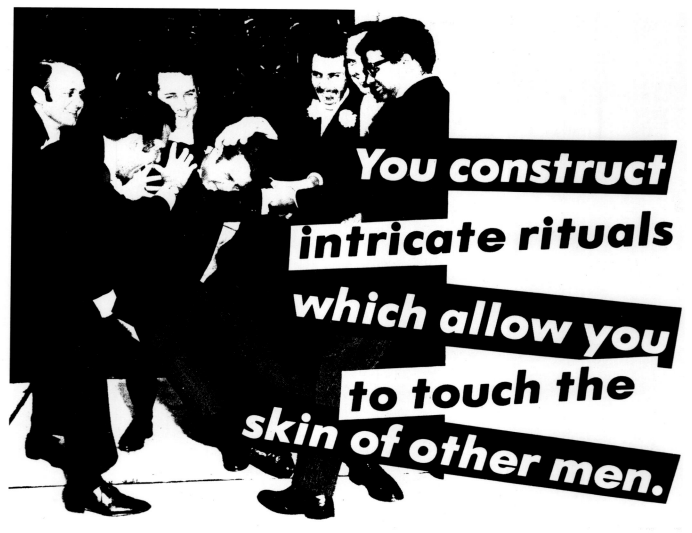

You construct intricate rituals which allow you to touch the skin of other men.

Your *manias become* **science**

You substantiate our

horror

Turned
Trick

Your body

is a

battleground

March on Washington
Sunday, April 9, 1989

Support Legal Abortion
Birth Control
and Women's Rights

On April 26 the Supreme Court will hear a case which the Bush Administration hopes will overturn the Roe vs. Wade decision, which established basic abortion rights. Join thousands of women and men in Washington D.C. on April 9. We will show that the majority of Americans support a woman's right to choose. In Washington: Assemble at the Ellipse between the Washington Monument and the White House at 10 am; Rally at the Capitol at 1:30 pm

Images and symbols for the woman cannot be isolated from images and symbols of the woman. . . . It is representation, the representation of feminine sexuality . . . which conditions how it comes into play.

—Jacques Lacan

Kruger's art is inconceivable outside of the feminist movement and the complex of social issues in the 1970s that conferred new visibility on women artists. Like Kruger, many women turned toward photography, opposing its simple mechanical means of picture taking with the masculine ethos of creativity that was celebrated in the traditional media of painting and sculpture. But if Kruger is a spokeswoman for feminism, she is also its barometer, for beginning in the early 1980s her work registers a profound change within the women's movement. At this time in the United States, and several years earlier in Europe, a specific branch of feminism began to express dissatisfaction with the equal-rights strategies that infused cultural politics in the 1970s. At issue was the failure of these strategies—based on eliminating discrimination and establishing equal access to institutional power—to disturb the ideological structures of which discrimination is symptomatic; attention was focused on their rigid and deterministic definition of sexuality as "natural," pregiven, or biological. Among Kruger's generation, gender was not regarded as an innate or "essential" condition, but rather as a construction produced through representation. Sexuality was regarded as the result of signification and semiotic effects, rather than of biology—a perspective that offers the possibility of changing our restrictive definitions of gender. Masculinity and femininity came to be seen as the products of adaptation to social standards of sexuality, in which the impact of signs play a determining role. In a manner with radical implications for the visual arts, discussions converged on the politics of the image.

These debates concerning the construction of gender informed the practices of a number of women artists, writers, and filmmakers, whose ideas were echoed by sympathetic critics. Besides Kruger, one can count among the ranks of those working in New York the artists Louise Lawler, Sherrie Levine, Silvia Kolbowski, Sarah Charlesworth, and Laurie Simmons, writers Carol Squiers and Lynne Tillman, video and installation artist Judith Barry, and such filmmakers as Yvonne Rainer and Chantal Akerman. Sharing their concerns was a group of British artists, including Mary Kelly and Victor Burgin, whose work was well known in New York. Reflected in these practices is the influence of European theory, in particular the writings of Foucault, Baudrillard, Julia Kristeva, and Jacques Lacan, whose account of the construction of sexuality in language, the paradigmatic system for all representation and discourse, was taken as offering an account of the way in which patriarchal values are assigned. Also significant were the writings of the philosopher Jacques Derrida, which comprise an extensive critique of Western representation and its central concepts of originality, authority, and selfhood. Most texts were read only generally or

"Love" is entangled with the question of woman's complicity: it may be the bribe which has persuaded her to agree to her own exclusion. It may be historically necessary to be momentarily blind to father-love; it may be politically effective to defend—tightly, unlucidly—against its inducements, in order for a "relation between the sexes," in order to rediscover some feminine desire, some desire for a masculine body that does not respect the Father's law.

—Jane Gallop
(*The Daughter's Seduction*. Ithaca: Cornell University Press, 1982)

Don't threaten me with love, baby. Let's just go walking in the rain.
—Billie Holliday

were disseminated through discussion; in fact, Kruger, like others, has voiced her concern not to "illustrate" theory. Nevertheless, crucial notions that circulated within theory about the relations among sexuality, meaning, and language found their way into these artists' works.

An important source was the British journal *Screen*, which during the 1970s and early 1980s published articles that applied continental theory to the analysis of mainstream films. In text after text, popular movies were analyzed as major vehicles of sexual indoctrination, as complex apparatuses that worked to "position" their viewers according to established codes of gender. If we note that in 1982 Kruger herself began to write criticism dealing with the sexual ideology of mainstream film, we can assume that the issues of sexual positioning and specularity were available to her.

Feminist film theory, like other psychoanalytical theory, draws impetus from Freud's reading of sexuality as an ordering or assignment, one that is always attained through the mediation of signs. For Freud, looking held the key to sexual identity; in a critical moment before the oedipal state, he wrote in *Three Essays on the Theory of Sexuality* (1905), the child's look establishes its mother, or another, as lacking the masculine organ and therefore inherently "less than" the male.[16] Sexual difference thus derives from a visible difference, which structures woman as "castrated" within the patriarchal order. Freud's concept, however, should not be interpreted as anatomical determinism, for the play of absence and presence is only significant insofar as it already has meaning within a formation of sexual difference: it is specific to patriarchy and to its particular attribution of values. Lacan extended Freud's concept, describing the phallus as the privileged signifier, or signifier of privilege, in our society. In the Lacanian system, the phallus is the mark around which subjectivity, social law, and the acquisition of language turn; human sexuality is assigned and, consequently, lived, according to the position one assumes as either having or not having the phallus and with it, access to its symbolic structures.

Freud and Lacan's accounts indicate the problematic position of the girl-child in the social order. Denied access to language, she cannot represent but is, instead, represented—hence the prevalence of images of women in our society. The French psychoanalyst Luce Irigaray has addressed this exclusion of women through a play on words, *"rien à voir équivaut à n'avoir rien"* (nothing to see/show equals having nothing), hinting at woman's consignment to otherness, to the realm of the disenfranchised.[17] Many works by Kruger address the theme of absence ("I am your almost nothing" states a work of 1983 and "You delight in the loss of others" says another of 1982). In a piece from 1983, an image of a woman is overlaid with the words "We construct the chorus of missing persons," alluding to the construction of woman as a *category* (page 51) defined by the phallic term. Elsewhere Kruger adopts the tone of a tease, collaging the proposition "Now you see us . . . Now you don't" to an image of a rubber stopper suspended above a drain. Here Kruger gives literal form to the definition of woman as incomplete, partial, not "whole," or, more bluntly, a "hole".

Feminist theory has extended this critique by addressing the eye's propensity for mastery, exposing it as a distinctly masculine prerogative. Thus, Irigaray observes that "investment in the look is not privileged in women as in men. More than the other senses, the eye objectifies and masters. It sets at a distance, maintains the distance. In our culture, the predominance of the look over smell, taste, touch, hearing, has brought about an impoverishment of bodily relations. . . . The moment the look dominates, the body loses its materiality." (Note, again, the theme of the body's reduction in its transformation into image.[18]) Several works by Kruger comment on the illusion of visual detachment, disclosing it as a tool of masculine aggression. Indeed, Kruger's art is invariably directed at the manner in which visual mastery becomes aligned with difference or, more pointedly, at the way in which representations position women as objects of the male gaze. For as the British writer John Berger has observed, these sexual positions become culturally inscribed, resulting in a hegemony of representations: "*Men act* and *women appear*. Men look at women. Women watch themselves being looked at."[19]

Freud commented on the impure pleasures of looking, observing that vision is always implicated in a system of control. In *Three Essays on the Theory of Sexuality*, he cited pleasure in looking as an independent drive, evident in children, where it assumes both active and passive forms. Thus, voyeurism gives pleasure by positioning oneself against another—submitting the other to a distanced and controlling gaze—while the desire to be both subject and object of the gaze characterizes exhibitionism. Adult life, Freud wrote, is marked by the social predominance of one form over the other. Lacan later distinguished between the narcissistic impulse, which consists of erotic investment in one's personal image, and the inherently sadistic pleasure of the voyeur. Representations do not actually produce these objectifying effects; instead, they reproduce and reinforce modes of mastery that are found in early psychic structures of control. Nevertheless, the social shaping of the scopic drive is manifest in the regimes of looking enforced through ideology. One can discern, for example, the narcissistic investments of consumption, which invoke an ideal self-image through the acquisition of objects. And one can note, on the other hand, the ideology of the spectacle as authorized by the dominant order, in which one part of society represents itself to the other, reinforcing domination. Woman's con-

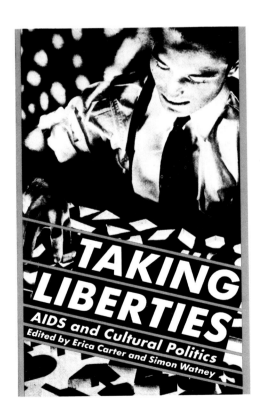

signment to this position of "otherness" is displayed across the panoply of social relations, appearing not only in aesthetic conventions (such as the female nude) but also in advertising, fashion photography, and the prescriptions of social decorum. Perhaps the clearest embodiment of this drive to master is found in popular film, where the dyad of passive woman versus active male is repeated (as Kruger mentions in her criticism) in the "silent stereotypical figure that settles the male gaze."[20]

Thus, when Kruger collages the words "Your gaze hits the side of my face" alongside the image of a stone female portrait head (page 62), she may be referring to the power of the gaze to arrest—literally petrify—its object (a tactic that Craig Owens has described as the "Medusa effect."[21] Elsewhere, she comments on this socialized immobility, configuring a subject held in place by dental appliances (the 1982 *You are a captive audience*). Here Kruger may also be referring to the convention in film and literary narrative by which the masculine protagonist arrests or advances action, controlling the course of events (a tendency she counters in one work with the admonition "You kill time"; page 49). Throughout her art women appear in static or supine poses, displayed according to clichéd conventions of popular representation. The binomial oppositions of active/passive, surveyor/surveyed, standing/supine, like the conceptual category culture/nature, are means by which society imposes its authority so as to subject one half to the privileged term. Although Kruger employs—even accentuates—these images, she suspends their masculine pleasures with the impertinences of superposed texts. When Kruger reproduces a photograph of a recumbent woman, her eyes significantly blinded by leaves, she disrupts its impositions with a feminist retort: "We won't play nature to your culture."

Kruger has stated her desire to "welcome the female spectator into the audience of men" and "to ruin certain representations." Her approach is directed toward an active viewer who can refuse or accept the address of the work. In keeping with contemporary feminist theory, she endorses Freud's refutation of the terms "masculine" and "feminine" in favor of active and passive *relations*, connecting sexuality to the situation of the subject. Another way of saying this is that masculinity and femininity are not absolutes but rather positions in language, whose values can only be determined through the set of relations in which they are inscribed. This concern with the "place" of the subject in representation is evident from Kruger's use in her art of the terms "I," "me," "we," and "you," which do not indicate objects that exist independently of discourse but instead suggest the positions of partners in a conversation. The linguist Roman Jakobson has designated these personal pronouns as "shifters," because their referents change place in the course of conversation, denoting differing relations of speaker and addressee.[22] In Kruger's hands, these pronouns

I long to become the best version of myself I can be . . . I want fantasy to appear and never go away; I want all my papers in order and clutter down to a bare minimum. I want to have already happened, and yet I love it just the way it is.

—Sandra Bernhard

(*Confessions of a Pretty Lady*. New York: Harper and Row, 1988)

work to dislocate the mastering effect of the image, showing that the viewer's place can shift, be indefinite, and refuse alignment with gender.

If sexual roles are constructed in representation, they can also be revised and restructured in discourse: thus, feminist theory contrasts the multiplicity of subject positions in language with the rigid paradigms of identity generated by and for the social order. The feminist approach to art and media has, in consequence, entailed a broad critique of signification, for all representations position their viewers, allowing for active participation in or subjection to meaning in an attitude of passive consumption. Since society depends on repetition to stabilize meanings, most images and texts confirm and duplicate subject positions. Consumption, therefore, sets the stage for ideological domination; as Barthes has suggested, the reproduction of the system

UNTITLED (WE DON'T NEED ANOTHER HERO). 1987.
Photographic silkscreen on vinyl, 108¾ × 157¾".
Courtesy Mary Boone Gallery, New York

UNTITLED (YOUR LIFE IS A PERPETUAL INSOMNIA).
1984.
Photograph, 72 × 48"

UNTITLED (YOU KILL TIME). 1983.
Photograph, 72 × 48".
Collection Chase Manhattan Bank, New York

UNTITLED (BUSY GOING CRAZY). 1989.
Photograph, 70 × 48".
Courtesy Mary Boone Gallery, New York

UNTITLED (ADMIT NOTHING/BLAME EVERYONE/BE
BITTER). 1987.
Photographic silkscreen on vinyl, 100⅜ × 179¾".
Collection Ydessa Hendeles Art Foundation,
Toronto

UNTITLED (ENDANGERED SPECIES). 1987.
Photographic silkscreen on vinyl, 107½ × 191½".
The Beckman Collection, New York

UNTITLED (WE CONSTRUCT THE CHORUS OF MISSING
PERSONS). 1983.
Photograph, 48 × 84".
Collection The Israel Museum, Jerusalem
Gift of Martin Sklar, New York

UNTITLED (YOUR MOMENTS OF JOY HAVE THE
PRECISION OF MILITARY STRATEGY). 1980.
Photograph, 37 × 50"
Courtesy Rhona Hoffman Gallery, Chicago

UNTITLED (YOU CONSTRUCT INTRICATE RITUALS
WHICH ALLOW YOU TO TOUCH THE SKIN OF OTHER
MEN). 1983.
Photograph, 38 × 50"

UNTITLED (YOUR MANIAS BECOME SCIENCE). 1981.
Photograph, 37 × 50".
Collection Dr. and Mrs. Peter Broido, Chicago

UNTITLED (YOU SUBSTANTIATE OUR HORROR). 1986.
Photograph, 144 × 96".
Collection Musée National d'Art Moderne
Centre Georges Pompidou, Paris

UNTITLED (GOD SENDS THE MEAT AND THE DEVIL
COOKS). 1988.
Photographic silkscreen on vinyl, 111 × 131½".
Collection Marc and Livia Straus

UNTITLED (FREE LOVE). 1988.
Photograph, 84 × 48".
Collection Gallery Bébert, Rotterdam, The
Netherlands

UNTITLED (TURNED TRICK). 1988.
Photographic silkscreen on vinyl, 122½ × 109".
Courtesy Mary Boone Gallery, New York

UNTITLED (YOUR BODY IS A BATTLEGROUND). 1989.
Poster for march on Washington, 29 × 24"

TAKING LIBERTIES. 1987.
Cover design by Barbara Kruger. Courtesy
Serpentine Press, London

UNTITLED (YOUR GAZE HITS THE SIDE OF MY FACE).
1981.
Photograph, 60 × 40".
Collection Vijak Mahdavi and Bernardo Nadal-
Ginard

UNTITLED (IF YOU CAN'T FEEL IT, IT MUST BE REAL).
1988.
Photograph, 51½ × 58½"

requires our consumption of its codes. In our capitalist world, characterized as it is by privatized forms of gratification, there is an increased investment in leisure goods and services that are far from simple organs of entertainment. The array of enticements these commodities offer cannot conceal the limited meanings they convey; instead, they extend the regime of control implemented through the signifier. Kruger encapsulates this fascination with a gloss from Walter Benjamin: we are "seduced by the sex appeal of the inorganic."

Money can buy you love

When I hear the word **culture** I take out my checkbook

We mouth your words

Buy

I'll change your life

me

Put your money where your mouth is

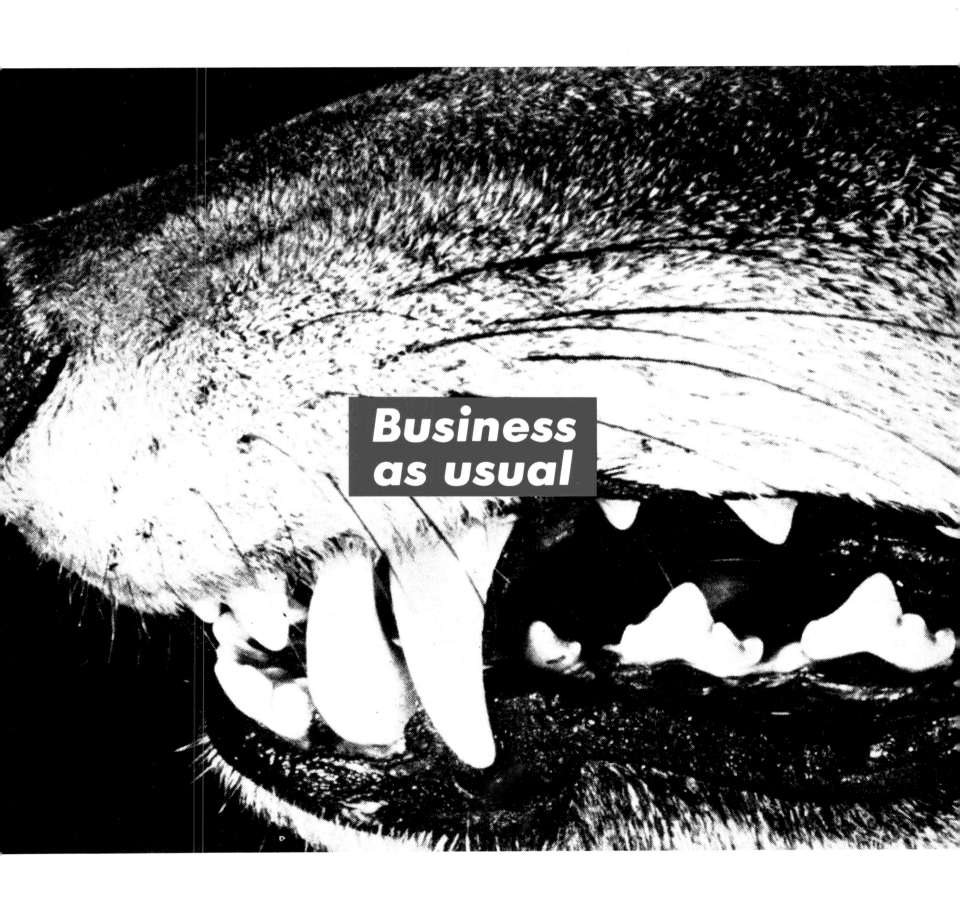

Business
as usual

Buy me. I'll change your life.

— **Barbara Kruger**

I n 1984 Kruger's work underwent a subtle change that confounded members of the art community. In a one-person exhibition organized that year, she showed two bodies of work, one the by-now well-known photocollages concerning women's relations to looking, the other a new series dealing, bluntly and assertively, with money. The central features in her work, down to the signature red frames, were all in evidence, but the focus of her pronomial play had shifted to a broader and more intricate sphere. For if the addressee in the early works was a masculine-sexed subject, the new series spoke to a more complex and reticulated group of interests, foregrounding money and consumption as guarantees of masculine power. In one work, drops of milk suspended from a baby's bottle are extended by the admonishment "You are getting what you paid for"; in another, an image of a grimacing bug-eyed toy is superposed with the commodity's exhortative lure, "Buy me. I'll change your life"; in a third work (page 69), the silence of the image of an exploding house is countered by the cryptic accusation "Your money talks" (page 72). Although the two series were interpreted separately, they disclose an underlying identity, hinging on the sign as a site of social, economic, and sexual control.

Kruger alluded to the masculine relations of the market in an article published that year in the magazine *Effects*, describing "the law of the father" as "the calculator of capital."[23] She ascribed the new prominence in her work of the theme of the market to a personal need, motivated by her increasing visibility in the art world, to comment critically on the marketplace, to be both *in* and *about* consumption. Her comments point to a broad development in recent art, evident from Andy Warhol to Jeff Koons, describing the market as the inescapable condition of contemporary production.

Kruger's critique of the sign as commodity brings to mind the writings of Jean Baudrillard, which were central to many contemporary artists. In a celebrated group of texts first published in the 1960s, Baudrillard elucidated a stage in social relations that is no longer marked by the Marxist ethos of production but by the ideology of consumption—or by consumption as the dominant ideology. Describing a breakdown in the Marxist opposition between the cultural and the economic, Baudrillard detailed the "commodification" of the former and "symbolization" of the latter. "Today," he argued, "consumption . . . defines precisely *the stage where the commodity is immediately produced as a sign, as sign value, and where signs (culture) are produced as commodities.*"[24] In this stage, in other words, the language of capital has so penetrated the sign that material production is indistinguishable from its semiotic effects. Consumption, Baudrillard tells us, is no longer dictated by needs or even by "real objects as sources of satisfaction," but by semiotic prestige. His aphorism—"the appearance of things has the keys to the city"—is less an indictment of our superficial

If the soul of the commodity . . . existed, it would be the most empathetic ever encountered in the realm of souls, for it would have to see in everyone the buyer in whose hand and house it wants to nestle.

—Walter Benjamin
(*Charles Baudelaire: A Lyric Poet in the Era of High Capitalism.* London: NLB, 1973)

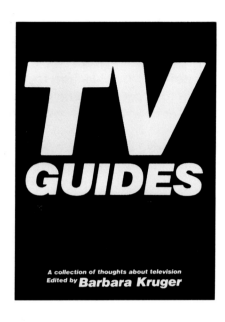

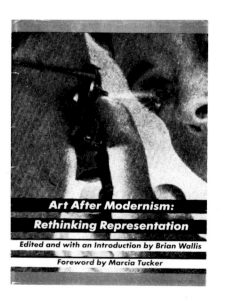

values than an invocation of a state in which power has receded into the manipulation of signs:

> Dominant classes have always either assured their domination over sign values from the outset . . . or endeavored (in the capitalist bourgeois order) to surpass, to transcend and to consecrate their economic privilege in a semiotic privilege, because this later stage represents the ultimate stage of domination. *This logic*, which comes to relay class logic and *which is no longer defined by ownership of the means of production but by the mastery of the process of signification* . . . activates a mode of production radically different from that of material production . . . [italics mine].[25]

Spectacle, then, represents a stage of display, and of manipulation through display, that manifests itself in control over the construction, distribution, and reception of information. This is the case with the dissemination of photographs, which function as the central channel through which sexual fantasies are circulated. And it is increasingly the case with television, which, Kruger notes in *TV Guides* (page 74), a collection of essays she edited, "dispenses power and its simulations."[26] Semiotic power informing our channels of communication was also the subject of two panel discussions that Kruger organized with Phil Mariani ("The Regulation of Fantasy: Sexuality, and the Law" and "Journalism and the Construction of the News") at the DIA Foundation in 1987. However, Kruger is not content simply to describe the ubiquitous coercions of signs; instead, she would expose the way in which consumption is endemic to a society that is romantic, patriarchal, and capitalist, driven by the urge for mastery (page 81).

The scope of mastery has been illuminated by Mark C. Taylor in *Erring*, a recent book on the postmodern that involves a discussion of the philosophical aspects of consumption. Noting the meanings of the verb *to consume* ("to take up completely, make away with, devour, lay hold of, burn, or reduce to ashes"), Taylor comments that the consumer's urge to appropriate otherness is not only boundless but also characteristic of our sense of self:

> The sovereign subject who seeks total mastery joins utility and consumption to form utilitarian consumerism. The result of this union is an economy of domination based on the principle of ownership. Ownership, in turn, presupposes both propriety and property. The accumulation of property is intended to secure the identity and insure the propriety of the hoarding self. When needy subjects seek satisfaction by consuming useful objects, the struggle for mastery expands into the economic domain. . . .[27]

Taylor, however, cautions us not to restrict this economy to "the money complex," for the principle of ownership is all-pervasive, appearing in the public sector as political colonialism or totalitarianism and in the private sphere as "phallocentric" sexuality. Everywhere the appropriative urge of consumption reflects a desire to organize lack, or master absence, that is embedded in the patriarchal unconscious. From which Taylor concludes that "mastery, utility, consumption, ownership, propriety, property, colonialism, and totalitarianism form a seamless, though seamy web."[28]

The ideology of consumption, then, is played out on several levels, each of which is manifested in Kruger's art. Thus, when Kruger accosts the viewer with the accusation "Your assignment is to divide and conquer" in one work, she refers both to the masculine desire to subjugate woman and to the political imperative to domesticate others, to colonize and control. For as Taylor reminds us, conquest has everything to do with self-possession ("the self that labors to establish its identity tries to surmount the threat that the other poses to its autonomy by dissolving alterity and assimilating difference. The act of aggression is simultaneously hostile and erotic"[29]). Works by Kruger project this theme as personal loss, instituted through sexual power (*Do I have to give up me to be loved by you?*; page 89). Others invoke the all-consuming urge for consumption (*Jam life into death*; page 95).

Kruger, however, does not neglect the more obvious aspects of consumption, evident in the commodity's insistent lures. In a 1986 catalog essay on Kruger's art, Baudrillard remarked on the publicity that is the counterpart to our modern public realm.[30] "Today," he writes, "all things . . . are condemned to publicity, to making themselves believable, to being seen and promoted . . . in the very heart of merchandise (and, by extension, in the very heart of our entire universe of signs), there is *an evil genius of advertising*, a trickster, who has integrated the buffoonery of merchandise with its mise-en-scène, its staging. An ingenious scriptwriter (perhaps capital itself) has pulled the world into a phantasmagoria, and we are all its spellbound victims."

Kruger's art reveals this self-publicizing aggrandizement on two levels. On one, it mimics the strategies of the commodity, invoking the snares and innuendos by which the viewer is beckoned and captivated. On the other, it replicates the tactics of commodity production, calling attention to "preparation and product, . . . [to] the refinements that accumulate to produce representation."[31] These tactical maneuvers are evident in Kruger's technical elaborations (cropping, enlarging, overprinting) and in her use of media, which ranges, most recently, from large silkscreened vinyl panels to the kind of moving plastic lenticular screens employed in greeting cards and

Money expresses the qualitative difference of things in terms of "how much?" Money, with all its colorlessness and indifference, becomes the common denominator of all values; irreparably it hollows out the core of things, their individuality, their specific value, and their incomparability.

—Georg Simmel
(*The Sociology of Georg Simmel*. New York: Macmillan, 1950)

75

souvenirs. Moreover, it is evident in her use of red enameled frames to commodify her images, announcing their market status and pointing to the market as the irrefutable condition that no object—least of all art—can evade.

No discussion of Kruger's examination of consumption is complete without mention of her written criticism and of the direct relationship it has to her visual art. Her writings fall into three general categories: critical articles, reviews on contemporary film and video published in *Artforum,* and a monthly column on television, dubbed "Remote Control," that she has authored for the same magazine since 1987. All of her texts address consumption as encountered in media projects (for example, in game shows, children's television, and mainstream and independent cinema) and all manifest a characteristic verbal style. It is a style that is at once idiosyncratic and typical, sumptuous and perverse, utilizing dense accumulations of metaphors garnered from media stereotypes. The constant rhetorical thickness simulates the entrapments of the commodity, for the style is excessive, bristling with signifiers. Like the commodity, its seductive impact can be overpowering. Still, Kruger's razor-thin edge of commentary enacts her characteristic program: seduce, dislocate, deter.

In these texts, the pacing of her thoughts moves rapidly, delineating the broad-reaching yet intricate mesh of relations circumscribing mass-media society. For example, in a review of Judith Barry's "Casual Shopper," a videotape that peruses the characteristic pleasures of the suburban female, Kruger moves from the particular to the general.[32] Citing Barry's use of a popular romantic tune ("Call me. Don't be afraid to just call me . . .") as background music, Kruger expatiates on the commodity's omnipresence: "Around everywhere, from the baroque shopping palaces of the late 19th century to the contemporary suburban merchandise behemoths. The pedestrian traffic within these structures resembles a carefully punctuated and at times graceful dance of acquisition performed against a familiar backdrop: the seamless exposition of the market commodity." This scenic contemporary landscape is marked both by its ubiquity and by its relationship to looking, to a "scopic exercise," intimately connected to the experience of desire, that connects shopping to the signifying systems of television and film. For Kruger notes that the motor of the woman's passionate quest is lack, or more specifically, the search for those objects that would comprise her image of completeness, as patriarchally defined. (Remarking on the appeal of possessions, Kruger quotes Benjamin: "If the soul of the commodity . . . existed, it would be the most empathetic encountered in the realm of souls, for it would have to see in everyone the buyer in whose hand and home it wants to nestle.")

In advertising, the signifiers of sex and money are displaced onto inanimate objects; hence it is not surprising that much of Kruger's "Remote Control" column is

You make history when you do business

devoted to delineating the techniques employed "to animate and sexualize the merchandise."[33] Here the fetishism of commodities segues with the promise of illusions, for we are truly seduced by the appeal of inorganic objects. Kruger, however, interprets merchandise in its broadest sense as including the entire realm of images, thereby encompassing the coercions of talk shows, news reporting, and politics. In each case, the pose wins out, evacuating all specificities and "unpleasant textualities" for the illusion of a smooth, untroubled whole.[34] Still, Kruger's writings do more than expose the discursive guises of power as it vacates "real" space for the image screen; they underline the invasion of the public realm, or publicity, into the private, and the commutation of the two terms. For the situation is one in which the social directives of our society are displaced, through television, from major institutional axes onto the circumscribed parameters of the home. Here, Kruger writes, the evil genius of advertising foregrounds "the home as the nexus of receivership, relocating visual and commercial reception."

> With television as the vector of control, expeditions "outside" become sporadic and predetermined. The nooks and crannies of social relations, from mercantile wranglings to romantic tussles, are ironed out into a smooth, seamless continuum of demiassociated moments. In addition, information has been transformed from a raw material into a highly directive demographic tool. The active collapses into the passive, and the increasingly archaic idea of volition is left loitering around one of the few enterprises still available to it: shopping.[35]

He entered shop after shop, priced nothing, spoke no word, and looked at all objects with a wild and vacant stare.
—Edgar Allen Poe
(The Man of the Crowd)

In a work Kruger made in 1987, a small hand holds up a placard emblazoned with the words, "I shop therefore I am." Defining consumption as the hallmark of identity, the gesture radicalizes Descartes's famous proposition, which installed consciousness as knowledge and, with it, instituted our modern sense of self. But in Kruger's hands this action does more than parody Descartes's *cogito*, which inscribed the human subject's predominance over surrounding objects through a propensity for thought. For here the individual is displaced from this central position by the object, which now establishes its priority, and sovereignty, over the subject: the consumer world, as Kruger remarks of "Pee-wee's Playhouse," is a place where *things* reign supreme.[36] Moreover, the body is depleted, eviscerated, its vulnerability "a liability compared to the promise of the smooth hum and unyielding surfaces of appliances."[37] The body's impurity and imperfection stand against the pristine wholeness of things that glisten and corruscate, announcing the luxury of their wares. Kruger's card, then, announces the body's incorporation into the systems that contain it. But mention must be made here of the shimmer of another object: art.

Much of the acclaimed art of the past decade has been produced within a sphere in which art's transformation into commodity has reduced its critical value, eroding the artist's adversarial stance. Today we know that Benjamin was historically limited: the conversion of art from cult value to exhibition value has not led the way to its political involvement, but rather to a transmutation of the major sites of aesthetic exchange into arenas for mercantile display. The increasing value of art as a tangible investment has resulted in the control of cultural representations by a moneyed class. True to Baudrillard, art's appearance as a highly marketable commodity has been accompanied by its manipulation as an item of power, publicity, prestige.

Kruger does not contest this; instead, her work is a comment on the process, an exposition of the fact that there are few alternatives to the market's relentless appropriations. Art appears within her work as the object of a controlled choreography of acquisition, one that is literalized in the shifting questions displayed on lenticular screens ("Can I help you?" "Can I interest you in something in red?" "Will that be cash or charge?"; page 91). But Kruger also indicates the futility of evasion through the fantasies of freedom promoted by idealist ideology. In fact, she indicates the way in which market value is developed precisely through time-worn romantic myths.

Her critique aims to intercept the codes that confer esthetic value—the notions of creativity, originality, and the "mastery" of the masterpiece that supply a sales pitch for aesthetic products. Kruger has repeatedly voiced her wish to "deconstruct the notion of the great artist" within its characteristic haunt, the gallery. She has also performed this sabotage in the museum, as in the exhibition "Picturing Greatness," which she curated for The Museum of Modern Art in 1987. In the accompanying wall labels Kruger parodied the "languages of 'greatness'" as "concocted with a slice of visual pleasure, a pinch of connoisseurship, a mention of myth and a dollop of money." Which is to say that artworks are often constructions designed to conceal the social nature of artistic activity (page 85).

When Kruger collages the remark "You produce an infinite sequence of originals" over the image of a woman drawing, she is referring to the way in which our concepts of representation depend on the regulation of scarcity. Although the valorization of the unique or singular over the debased copy is inherited from Romantic ideology, the contemporary market has employed it to its own ends to produce the illusion of rarity. Technically, the original is temporally located close to the origin—that is, to the moment of "creation" of the work—and its guarantee of authenticity is the stamp of the artist's hand. As Baudrillard observed in an article entitled "Gesture and Signature," the signature acts as the "sign among signs" to retain "the legendary values" of artistic creation;[38] similarly, it marks the work as private property, a commodity that the artist is legally entitled to exchange. Tellingly, Baudrillard links the signature to the French term for vintage, *appellation controllée*, emphasizing the notion of the propriety of property that resides within the proper name. Like others of her generation, Kruger rejects the notion of authenticity by appropriating images, which, being "anonymous," have no author and, hence, little authority. Similarly, her use of mechanical reproduction contrasts the serial, or multiple, with the uniqueness associated with products of the hand. For Kruger refuses the mystique of the unique object: the hand in her work is never singular, always social.

In *You invest in the divinity of the masterpiece* (page 19), Kruger appropriated the image from the Sistine Ceiling in which God reaches out to touch the hand of Adam, bestowing on him the gift of creation. The work is at once an indictment of art's commodity status, a comment on the aesthetic metaphor of the hand, and an exposition of the (masculine) ethos of artistic production as a transaction between fathers and sons. These themes are also implicit in a piece from 1984 in which the words "Your creation is divine/Our reproduction is human" appear over an Old Master drawing, exposing artistic value as a domain of masculine privilege and prestige. Here Kruger foregrounds the sexual hierarchy of artistic practice, just as she contraposes the serial, inherently social, nature of mechanical reproduction with the uniqueness connected to hand-crafted objects.

Kruger's assault on sexist mythologies is clearest in a billboard proclaiming "We don't need another hero" that was recently mounted in Los Angeles, Chicago,

A descriptive analysis of bank notes is needed. . . . The innocent cupids frolicking about numbers, the goddesses holding tablets of the law, the stalwart heroes sheathing their swords before monetary units, are a world of their own: ornamenting the façade of hell.

—Walter Benjamin
(Reflections. New York: Harcourt Brace Jovanovich, 1978)

New York, and Las Vegas, as well as cities in Australia, New Zealand, Ireland, and Great Britain. Against an image of a girl upbraiding a little boy who flexes his muscles in a "macho" exercise of power, Kruger frames an accusation that resonates on several levels, invoking our masculine model of artistic subjectivity, the artist-soldier figure of the avant-garde, and the increasing militarism of national patriotic values.[39] In this manner, she reveals the urge toward mastery, or sovereign individuality, as it operates in multiple domains. Yet her use of plural and often recondite sites also challenges the aesthetic reign of the proper name. For who in these distant locations, far removed from the art world and fronting on the highway, has ever pondered the significance of a "Barbara Kruger?"

Friday, March 27 8pm   The DIA Art Foundation presents 2 nights of panel discussions

Sexuality and the Law

The Regulation of Fantasy

Barbara Ehrenreich
moderator—Co-editor of "Re-Making Love" and contributor to
"The Mean Season: The Attack on the Welfare State"

Ann Snitow
—Co-editor of "Powers of Desire: The Politics of Sexuality"

Carole Vance
—Editor of "Pleasure and Danger: Exploring Female Sexuality"

Simon Watney
—Author of "Policing Desire: Pornography, Aids and the Media"

Saturday, March 28 8pm

Journalism and the Construction of the News

Christopher Hitchens
moderator—Columnist for The Nation and US Magazine

Dennis Bernstein and Robert Knight
—Producers of "Contra-gate", WBAI

Susan Meiselas
—Photo journalist and author of "Nicaragua: June 1978 - July 1979"

Joanne Omang
—Journalist, The Washington Post

Geoffrey Stokes
—"Press Clips", The Village Voice

DIA Art Foundation 155 Mercer St. NY 431-9232   Admission: $4.00
Organized by Barbara Kruger and Phil Mariani

The Nicaragua Media Project

Sept. 21 - Nov. 25, 1984
The New Museum Of Contemporary Art
583 Broadway, New York City

U.S. Marines in Nicaragua (c.1914)

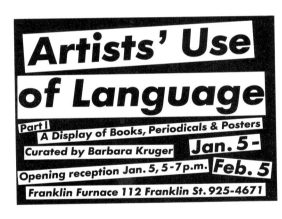

Artists' Use of Language

Part I
A Display of Books, Periodicals & Posters
Curated by Barbara Kruger   Jan. 5 -
Opening reception Jan. 5, 5-7 p.m.   Feb. 5
Franklin Furnace 112 Franklin St. 925-4671

Committed

Starring
Sheila McLaughlin
Victoria Boothby
Lee Breuer
John Erdman

Directed and Produced by
Sheila McLaughlin and Lynne Tillman
Camera, lenses and Written by Lynne Tillman
Cinematography by Heinz Emigholz
Music by Phillip Johnston

Remaking History

Discussions in Contemporary Culture
Dia Art Foundation October 1987 through May 1988

Cornel West
writer and cultural critic, Distinguished Professor of Philosophy
and Christian Practice, Union Theological Seminary, New York
October 22, 1987

Gayatri Spivak
author of "In Other Worlds: Essays in Cultural Politics," writer on
colonial discourse and cultural imperialism
November 18, 1987

Victoria de Grazia
historian of contemporary Europe, author of "The Culture of
Consent: The Organization of Leisure in Fascist Italy"
December 15, 1987

Bernard Tschumi
chief architect of the Parc de la Villette in Paris, architectural
theorist
January 19, 1988

Janet Abu-Lughod
urbanist and historian, author of "Rabat: Urban Apartheid in
Morocco"
February 9, 1988

Judith Williamson
media critic, author of "Decoding Advertisement" and "Consuming
Passions," a collection of essays
March 15, 1988

Edward Said
Parr Professor of English and Comparative Literature, Columbia
University, author of "The Question of Palestine" and "Orientalism"
April 19, 1988

J. Hoberman
film critic for "The Village Voice" and co-author of "Midnight
Movies"
May 10, 1988

Lectures will be held at 155 Mercer Street, New York City, and
will begin at 6:30 pm Admission: $4.00 per evening   431-9232
Organized by Barbara Kruger and Phil Mariani

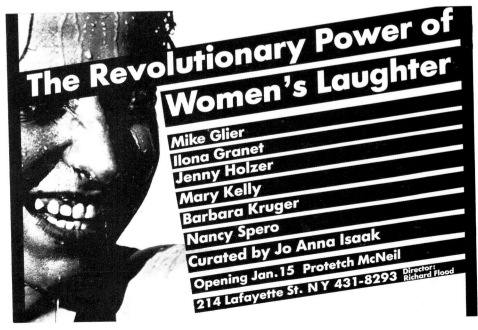

The Revolutionary Power of Women's Laughter

Mike Glier
Ilona Granet
Jenny Holzer
Mary Kelly
Barbara Kruger
Nancy Spero
Curated by Jo Anna Isaak
Opening Jan. 15 Protetch McNeil
214 Lafayette St. NY 431-8293   Director: Richard Flood

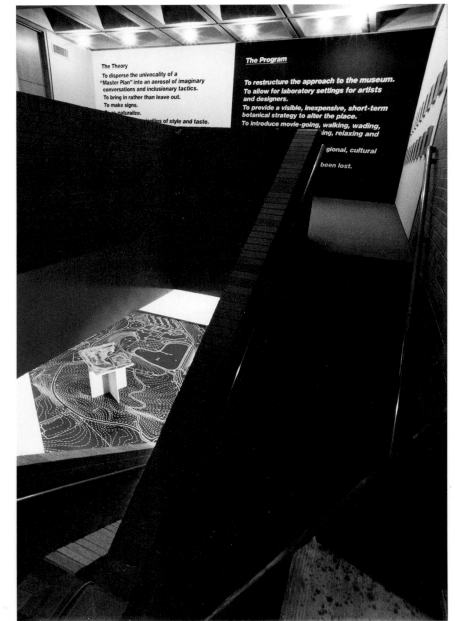

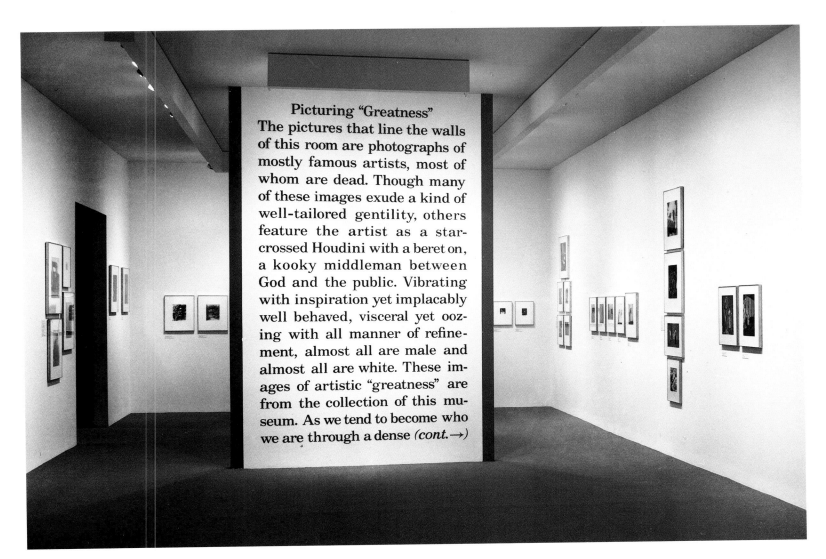

Picturing "Greatness"
The pictures that line the walls of this room are photographs of mostly famous artists, most of whom are dead. Though many of these images exude a kind of well-tailored gentility, others feature the artist as a star-crossed Houdini with a beret on, a kooky middleman between God and the public. Vibrating with inspiration yet implacably well behaved, visceral yet oozing with all manner of refinement, almost all are male and almost all are white. These images of artistic "greatness" are from the collection of this museum. As we tend to become who we are through a dense *(cont.→)*

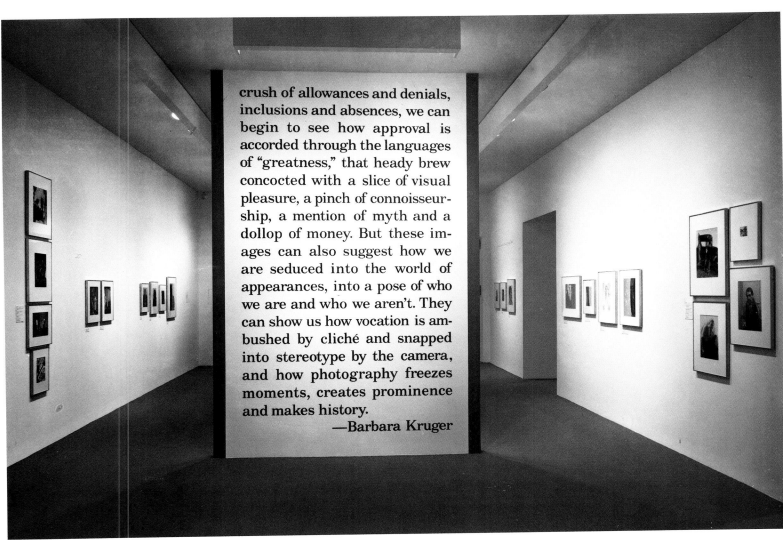

crush of allowances and denials, inclusions and absences, we can begin to see how approval is accorded through the languages of "greatness," that heady brew concocted with a slice of visual pleasure, a pinch of connoisseurship, a mention of myth and a dollop of money. But these images can also suggest how we are seduced into the world of appearances, into a pose of who we are and who we aren't. They can show us how vocation is ambushed by cliché and snapped into stereotype by the camera, and how photography freezes moments, creates prominence and makes history.
—Barbara Kruger

This afternoon I am visited by Kruger, weary from a night spent covering walls in lower Manhattan with posters. We converse briefly on the perils of postering—one's efforts are always being sabotaged by rival brigades—then Kruger shows me two recent images designed for political efforts. One is for an AIDS fund-raising campaign in San Francisco. On it, two hands (again, a social gesture) are clasped so as to suggest equivocal readings; a sign of solidarity and, alternately, an image of combat come to mind. But I am drawn most readily to the other poster, the object of Kruger's nocturnal duties (pages 58). Designed in support of abortion rights and targeted for the April 9, 1989, march on Washington (a march that would call attention to the Supreme Court hearing on a case that might overturn the landmark *Roe* v. *Wade* decision), the image shows a woman's face, its contours dramatically foreshortened and cropped close at hairline and chin. The face is styled according to the fashions of the 1950s, but, more importantly, it is divided, split along its vertical axis into an image and its photographic negative. The poster summons up conventional oppositions—positive versus negative, white versus black, good versus bad. Yet here there is no Picassoid play, for Kruger is deadly serious: across the surface is inscribed, "Your body is a battleground."

By invoking a well-known slogan from the 1960s, Kruger makes use of the stereotype; that the female body is a site of struggle is, by now, conventional wisdom. However, the slogan points to a direction in her recent work, which is addressed less to the body as incorporated than to the corporeal body, the body that inhabits the space and time of lived life, in all its sensuous particularity. Her recent pieces make tangible an effort to reinscribe this living, breathing body into the locations denied it by ideology, reversing the stereotype's disembodied address and countering the reductiveness of the image. For Kruger, this recovery of the body's multiplicity has a strategic aim, for in multiplicity is the key to mutability, to social transformation, and to change.

This aim is reflected throughout Kruger's repertory of visual devices, all of which affirm the body's capacities. Several works from 1989 employ textured pictures, drawn from nineteenth-century engravings, that confer a new tactility on her art, while others achieve a Braille-like palpability through the variegated surfaces of incised magnesium plates. Some employ the multiple positions required by lenticular screens to choreograph the body's activities (page 91). Others invoke the theme of corporeal loss: thus, the image of a surgeon removing the heart from a woman is countered by the car owner's caveat to robbers, "No radio" (page 39). This theft of the body's motor—and hence, of its claims to experience—is inflected in another register in a work that inscribes the query "Do I have to give up me to be loved by you?" (page 89), across the throbbing interior of a heart. The work's carnal specificity negates the slickness of the mediated image much as its proposition offsets the masculine incorporation of emotion and feeling. In these works Kruger proposes new strategies of interference. We have discovered the coercions of the media; we must develop the means by which we would confront them.

MY PRETTY PONY. 1988.
by Stephen King and Barbara Kruger.
Limited edition published by the Library Fellows of
the Whitney Museum of American Art. Photographs
by Philip Pocock

Notes

1. Unless otherwise noted, all quotations from Kruger's statements are taken from conversations with the author or from published interviews. The latter include Kate Linker, "Barbara Kruger Interview," *Flash Art*, March 1985, pp. 36–37; Gary Indiana, "Untitled (Are we having fun yet?)," *The Village Voice*, May 26, 1987, p. 99; Jeanne Siegal, "Barbara Kruger: Pictures and Words," *Arts Magazine*, June 1987, pp. 17–20; and Anders Stephanson, "Barbara Kruger," *Flash Art*, October 1987, pp. 55–59.

2. Much of my biographical information is drawn from Carol Squiers's excellent article, "Diversionary (Syn)tactics: Barbara Kruger Has Her Way with Words," *Art News*, February 1987, pp. 76–85.

3. Ibid., p. 81.

4. Michel Foucault, *Discipline and Punish: The Birth of the Prison* (New York: Pantheon, 1977), p. 26.

5. Ibid., p. 25.

6. Foucault, *Power, Truth, Strategy*, edited by Meaghan Morris and Paul Patton (Sydney: Feral Publications, 1979), p. 36.

7. This insight, noted by Norman Bryson in his *Vision and Painting: The Logic of the Gaze* (New Haven: Yale University Press, 1983), pp. 150–52, has also been cited by Craig Owens in "The Medusa Effect, or The Spectacular Ruse" in *We won't play nature to your culture. Works by Barbara Kruger* (London: Institute of Contemporary Art, 1983), p. 7.

8. Bryson, p. 159.

9. Ibid., pp. 159–161.

10. Ibid., p. 150.

11. Roland Barthes, "Lecture in Inauguration of the Chair of Literary Semiology, Collège de France," *October* 8 (Spring 1979), p. 5.

12. Owens, op. cit., p. 7.

13. See Bryson, op. cit., pp. 155–156.

14. Jacques Attali, *Noise: The Political Economy of Music* (Minneapolis: University of Minnesota Press, 1985), p. 87.

15. Jean Baudrillard, "The Ecstasy of Communication," in *The Anti-Aesthetic: Essays on Postmodern Culture*, edited by Hal Foster (Seattle, Bay Press, 1983), p. 126.

16. For further discussion of the influence of psychoanalytic theory on contemporary artistic practice, see my "Representation and Sexuality," *Parachute* 32 (Fall 1983), pp. 12–23, and the texts collected in *Difference: On Representation and Sexuality*; edited by Kate Linker (New York: The New Museum of Contemporary Art, 1985).

17. Luce Irigaray, *Speculum of the Other Woman* (Ithaca: Cornell University Press, 1985), p. 48.

18. Interview with Irigaray in *Les femmes, la pornographie, l'érotisme*, edited by M.-F. Hans and G. Lapouge (Paris, 1978), p. 50, as cited in Owens, "Feminists and Postmodernism," in *The Anti-Aesthetic*, p. 70.

19. John Berger, *Ways of Seeing* (London: Penguin, 1977), p. 47.

20. Barbara Kruger, "Virtue and Vice on 65th Street," *Artforum*, January 1983, p. 66.

21. Owens, op. cit.

22. For a discussion of the linguistic use of the shifter, see Owens, op. cit., and Rosalind Krauss, "Notes on the Index: Seventies Art in America," *October* 3 (Spring 1977), p. 69.

23. Kruger, "Incorrect," *Effects* 2 (1984), p. 18.

24. Baudrillard, "Toward a Critique of the Political Economy of the Sign," in Baudrillard, *For a Critique of the Political Economy of the Sign* (Saint Louis: Telos Press, 1981), p. 147.

25. Baudrillard, "The Art Auction," ibid., pp. 115–116.

26. Kruger, ed., *TV Guides. A collection of thoughts about television* (New York: The Kuklapolitan Press, 1985), p. 35.

27. Mark C. Taylor, *Erring: A Postmodern A/theology* (Chicago and London: University of Chicago Press, 1987), p. 27.

28. Ibid., p. 28.

29. Ibid., p. 30.

30. Baudrillard, "Untitled," in *Barbara Kruger* (New York: Mary Boone/Michael Werner Gallery, 1987), n.p.

31. Kruger, review of *The Golden Eighties*, directed by Chantal Akerman, in *Artforum*, December 1983, p. 84.

32. Kruger, review of "Casual Shopper" by Judith Barry, in *Artforum*, March 1983, p. 73.

33. Kruger, "Remote Control," *Artforum*, January 1987, p. 10.

34. Kruger, "Remote Control," *Artforum*, September 1987, p. 9.

35. Kruger, "Remote Control," *Artforum*, January 1987, p. 10.

36. Kruger, "Remote Control," *Artforum*, March 1987, p. 10.

37. Kruger, "Game Show," *Real Life*, October 1979, p. 5.

38. Baudrillard, "Gesture and Signature" in *For a Critique of the Political Economy of the Sign*, op. cit., p. 105.

39. For a discussion of this billboard project and related works, see Owens, "From Work to Frame, Or Is There Life after 'The Death of the Author'," in *Implosion: A Postmodern Perspective* (Stockholm: Moderna Museet, 1987), p. 209.

The image . . . always has the last word. —*Roland Barthes*
(*Barthes by Barthes*. New York: Hill and Wang, 1977)

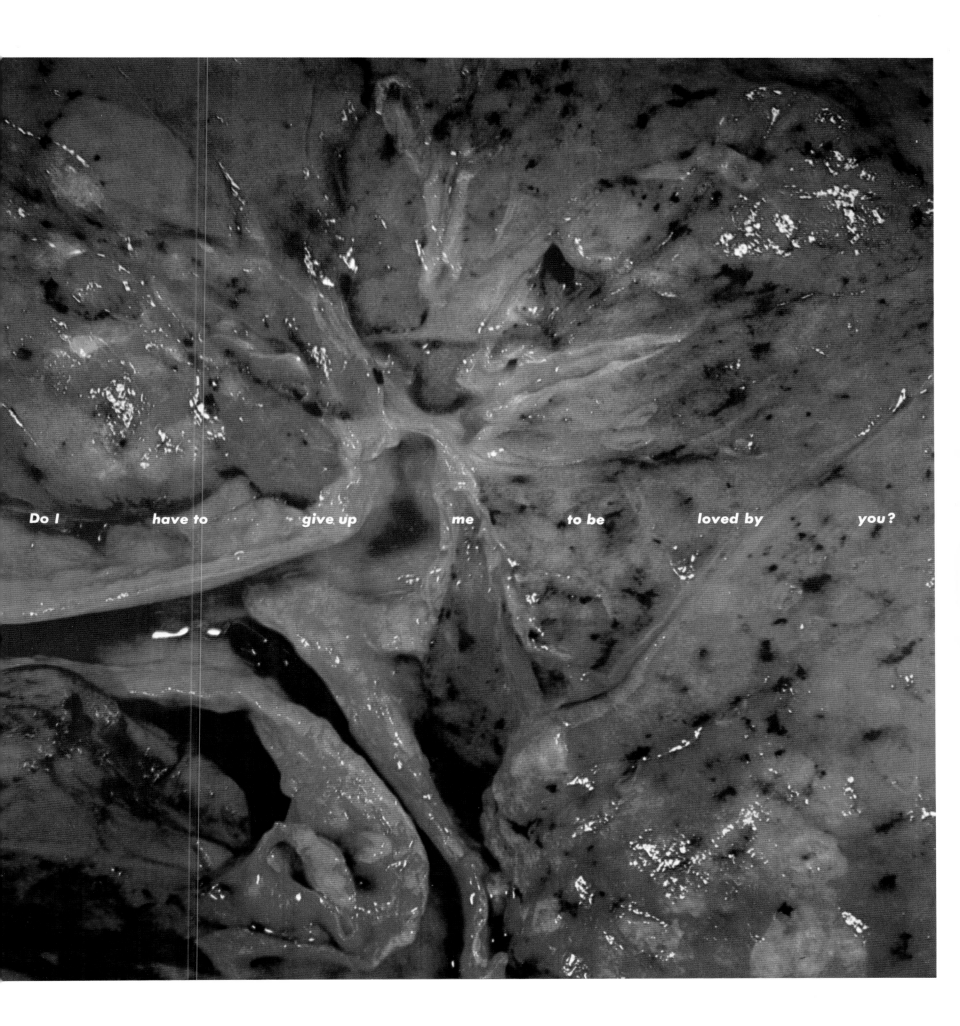

Do I   have to   give up   me   to be   loved by   you?

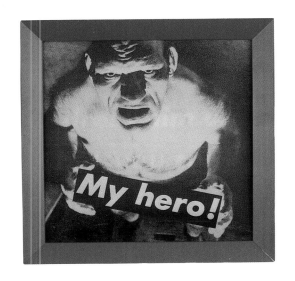

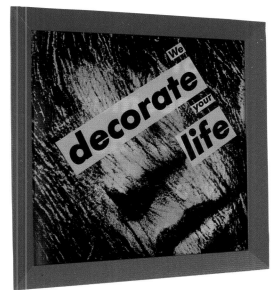

There is only

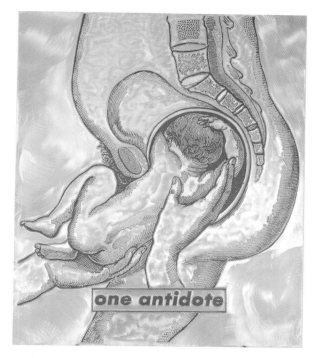

one antidote

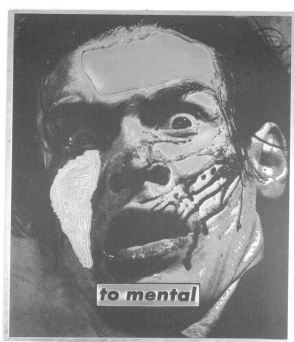

to mental

suf'fer *v.t.* [OF. *sufrir, sofrir,* fr. L. *sufferre,* fr. *sub-* + *ferre* to bear.] **1.** To submit to or be forced to endure; bear as a victim or patient (sense 3). **2.** To undergo; experience; pass through; as, to *suffer* alteration. **3.** To have power to resist or sustain;—chiefly in negative statements; as, not able to *suffer* the cold. **4.** To allow; permit; tolerate; put up with; as, to *suffer* fools gladly. —*v.i.* **1.** To undergo pain of body or mind. **2.** *Archaic.* To endure or tolerat **suffering** njury, etc. **3.** To sustain loss or damage.

and that is

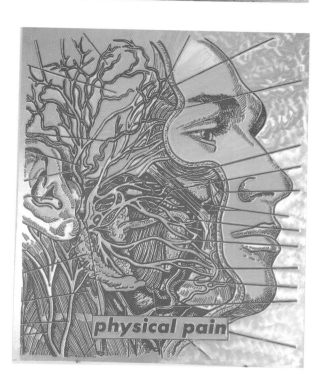

physical pain

JAM
LIFE
INTO
DEATH

Remember
Me